Praise for *Make Peace with Your Mind*

"When I first met Mark Coleman at a retreat at the Spirit Rock Meditation Center, I immediately appreciated the clarity he brought to his teachings. This book is written in the same clear voice, providing an easy-to-follow road map to understanding and defeating our inner critic."

— Troy Aikman, Pro Football Hall of Fame quarterback and Fox Sports broadcaster

"Mark Coleman has written a wonderful and important book. If we can make friends with ourselves, we activate the place inside that has always truly wanted our well-being. Transforming the mind from inner critic to best friend is the key to a more fulfilling life. *Make Peace with Your Mind* is the perfect guidebook to help us do just that. An excellent offering!"

— James Baraz, coauthor of *Awakening Joy* and cofounding teacher at Spirit Rock Meditation Center, Woodacre, California

"Mark Coleman has written a wonderfully original book, addressing the inner critic that keeps us from our most creative work. He understands that it is often buried deep, and he gives us a wide range of excavation tools, all of which are kind and helpful. Useful for anyone, I will use it especially with college students and young artists and professionals, whose external lives are full of judgments, as well as activists, who feel they can never do enough. This book is a great gift."

— Mirabai Bush, senior fellow at the Center for Contemplative Mind in Society, author of *Contemplative Practices for Higher Education*, and coauthor (with Ram Dass) of *Compassion in Action*

"Most of us wait for some champion to show up in our life who supports our dreams, calms our fears, and provides a vision for our future. Mark Coleman reminds us we can be our own champion by building a healthier relationship with our judgmental mind with clear and practical steps. This book can change your life."

— Chip Conley, *New York Times*–bestselling author of *Emotional Equations* and Head of Global Hospitality and Strategy at Airbnb

"In clear and powerful and terms, Mark Coleman offers readers highly practical tools to cultivate lasting calm, contentment, and happiness in any life circumstance. The tools outlined in this book will help readers confront one of the most persistent sources of difficulty anyone may encounter: one's own negative mind states. *Make Peace with Your Mind* is a uniquely transformational work offered to us by one of the world's preeminent mindfulness and meditation teachers. It is a must-read for anyone interested in meaningful personal growth and fulfillment."

— Rich Fernandez, PhD, cofounder of Wisdom Labs

"A beautiful guide to liberating our minds from endless cycles of self-criticism and creating the inner peace that leads to an exemplary life."

— Stephen Dinan, bestselling author of *Sacred America, Sacred World* and CEO of the Shift Network

"As we now know, the world inside and the world outside are not so different — and the sneakily destructive inner critic can make a mess of self, other, and the whole world. In *Make Peace with Your Mind*, therapist, consultant, and Buddhist teacher Mark Coleman does as good a job as I have seen of explaining, deconstructing, and working with the inner critic, until she or he becomes an ally. The book includes many useful exercises for putting its important message into practice: that you need not go on with this misery any longer."

— Norman Fischer, Zen priest and author of *What Is Zen* and *Experience*

"Mark Coleman, an experienced therapist and a profound practitioner and teacher of meditation, has crafted an exquisite path toward peace and freedom with one of the most troubling aspects of our humanity: our inner critic. Drawing upon ancient wisdom traditions, contemporary psychological breakthroughs, and many other sources, Mark weaves these wisdom strands together into a fully accessible practical approach, illustrated with many examples and supported with practices that can build insight and competence. A marvelous guidebook brought to life by a warm, compassionate friend."

— James Flaherty, author of *Coaching: Evoking Excellence in Others* and founder of New Ventures West and Integral Leadership

"Drawing on decades of experience of freeing himself and others from the inner critic, Mark Coleman has written a beautiful, inspiring, and practical book for all who wish to find a way out from under the weight of their inner critic. Filled with wisdom and compassion, this book is a warm-hearted guide for applying mindfulness and common sense to alleviate the burden of the inner critic."

— Gil Fronsdal, guiding teacher at Insight Meditation Center and translator of *The Dhammapada*

"In his new book, *Make Peace with Your Mind*, Mark Coleman shares his own deep understanding of the often pervasive inner critic, and he offers many tools and methods for freeing ourselves from this common habit of mind. His clear style and compassionate wisdom combine to make this book a valuable support on our journey to freedom."
— Joseph Goldstein, author of *Mindfulness*

"This book is a rare combination of practical help, emotional support, compelling personal story, scientific foundations, and spiritual insight. Mark Coleman shows us how to let go of feeling pressured, inadequate, or afraid to express ourselves fully — and instead feel strong, confident, and worthy. A beautiful, soulful, enormously useful book."
— Rick Hanson, PhD, author of *Buddha's Brain*

"Both insightful and helpful, with gifts of wisdom and many practical tools to work with your own mind and heart."
— Jack Kornfield, author of *A Path with Heart* and cofounding teacher at Spirit Rock Meditation Center, Woodacre, California

"In this well-written book, Mark Coleman presents his personal reflections on how to free yourself from harsh self-criticism, based on his experience as a meditation teacher, coach, and therapist. With pragmatic exercises designed to help you better understand your own inner critic, this is a truly worthwhile read."
— Kristin Neff, associate professor at UT Austin and author of *Self-Compassion*

"The inner critic stops all growth, diminishes our life force, and crushes our soul. With kindness and clarity, Mark Coleman gives us proven practices to tame the critic's wild ways and access the more reliable guidance of true wisdom. Everybody's got an inner critic, so everybody needs a wise book like this one." — Frank Ostaseski, author of *The Five Invitations*

"In *Make Peace with Your Mind*, Mark Coleman gently guides us to work with the ubiquitous demon of self-judgment. His kind and clear writing style invites us to see and skillfully relate to this familiar human habit. Through teaching, story, and guided exercises, he inspires us to develop keen and compassionate relationships to the parts of ourselves that often seek to demean or even destroy our self-worth. He offers us the possibility of not only hope but genuine healing. This book on the critic will support anyone who desires stopping the inner war and developing holistic integration with all parts of themselves." — Sarah Powers, author of *Insight Yoga*

"Mark Coleman's *Make Peace with Your Mind* is a great read for all those looking to mindfulness to help them live their best life. Sometimes when life speeds up, it is best to take a few moments to slow down! The benefits of these practices are real and wide-ranging, and it is never too late to start." — Congressman Tim Ryan

"What I most love about *Make Peace with Your Mind* is the range of accessible practices it offers. From his own experience over many years, Mark Coleman has distilled powerful, creative strategies for relating with and transforming your inner critic. It's a wonderful, delightful, and deeply touching book." — Sharon Salzberg, author of *Lovingkindness* and *Real Happiness*

"*Make Peace with Your Mind* is a beautiful book that can help free you from the limited definitions of self-loathing and pain. I have known Mark Coleman for many years, and he is humble and wise and lives with an open heart — one who truly walks his talk. Mark's guidance is both wise and compassionate to support deep healing." — Bob Stahl, PhD, coauthor of *A Mindfulness-Based Stress Reduction Workbook* and *MBSR Everyday*

"Through Mark Coleman's decades of experience in mindfulness practices, he's unearthed tools that can help us with our inner critic — the voice that whispers to us and keeps us lost in self-doubt and old thought patterns. This book is a breath of fresh air, a path out of these cycles, and a way to help liberate us from our suffering in self-doubt." — Janet Stone, founder of Janet Stone Yoga

"This immensely practical book by meditation teacher and therapist Mark Coleman is a thorough and compassionate guide to working with the often relentless inner critic. Filled with stories from his own experience and the hundreds of people he has worked with over three decades, Mark brings wisdom, humor, kindness, and a vast repertoire of exercises that can change your life *now*!" — Diana Winston, director of Mindfulness Education at UCLA Mindful Awareness Research Center and author of *Fully Present*

MAKE PEACE WITH YOUR MIND

MAKE
PEACE
WITH YOUR
MIND

HOW MINDFULNESS AND COMPASSION
CAN FREE YOU FROM YOUR
— INNER CRITIC —

MARK COLEMAN

New World Library
Novato, California

New World Library
14 Pamaron Way
Novato, California 94949

The material in this book is intended for education. It is not meant to take the place of diagnosis and treatment by a qualified medical practitioner or therapist. No express or implied warranty of the effects of using the recommendations in this book can be given, nor any liability assumed.

All names and likenesses to real persons and companies have been changed.

Text design by Tona Pearce Myers

Library of Congress Cataloging-in-Publication Data is available.

First printing, November 2016
ISBN 978-1-60868-430-4
Ebook ISBN 978-1-60868-431-1
Printed in Canada on 100% postconsumer-waste recycled paper

 New World Library is proud to be a Gold Certified Environmentally Responsible Publisher. Publisher certification awarded by Green Press Initiative. www.greenpressinitiative.org

10   9   8   7   6   5   4   3   2   1

CONTENTS

———◄ ►———

PART 2. UNDERSTANDING SELF-JUDGMENT

PART 3. HOW TO WORK MINDFULLY WITH THE CRITIC

PART 4. THE POWER OF LOVE

PART 5. BEYOND THE CRITIC

FOREWORD

Stopping the war against ourselves is the key to healing our wounds and opening our hearts to the world. Yet putting down our weapons and learning to love our own being may be the greatest challenge we face in life. The inner voice of judgment and criticism can be unrelenting and painfully convincing as an arbiter of truth.

Mark Coleman's new book, *Make Peace with Your Mind*, offers a revealing look at this culturally pervasive and toxic habit we have of demeaning ourselves, and it offers a path of healing and freedom. A wise and caring therapist and meditation teacher, Mark deeply understands the intricacies of self-judgment and how the belief that something is wrong with us can prevent us from realizing the intimacy, creativity, and aliveness we seek.

Drawing on a dynamic weave of mindfulness, self-compassion, and potent experiential therapeutic strategies, Mark has helped thousands of people awaken to genuine self-love and to their intrinsic goodness. The wisdom of decades of skillful work is what he offers you in this book — a path that will radically transform your relationship with your innermost self.

In this clear and accessible book, you have a companion to guide and support you in stepping beyond the prison of feeling deficient and unworthy. Please give yourself the gift of taking the first step, of deepening your commitment to loving the life that is right here. And then, as you engage with these powerful teachings and meditation practices, you'll discover an openheartedness that includes all life everywhere.

With loving blessings,

Tara Brach

HOW I DISCOVERED THE CRITIC AND FOUND A WAY OUT

*I work early in the morning, before my nasty critic gets up — he rises
about noon. By then, I've put in much of a day's work.*

— VIRGINIA WOOLF

In my late teens I was a young man with a lot of rage. I was a
punk rocker, an anarchist, and in constant search of a target for
my anger. The punk rock and antiestablishment movements in the
political underground in London were perfect outlets for my fury.
Mostly it was directed toward the government, corporations, and
injustice. You could say they were easy targets.

What I didn't understand was that I had unconsciously become the target of much of my own hatred. My mind was filled
with self-flagellation, and through that murky lens I was never
good or smart enough. That deficiency tune was a mantra that played over and over in my head. Every decision, every
move, was wrong, stupid, or hopeless from my inner critic's point
of view.

I had rejected much of what I was told I should seek or want — academic achievement, status, wealth, even the recreational drugs my friends were bingeing on. But I was still seeking. The search is always hard when you don't know exactly what you are looking for. Yet sometimes life reminds us that the answer is closer than we think. And so it was that I fell into a path of mindfulness meditation that I discovered literally around the corner from the house where I was illegally squatting. It was to provide the answers my soul had longed for.

This inner journey began when I stumbled into what was back then, in 1984, a pretty rare thing — a meditation center in the heart of London's run-down East End. The moment I walked into the center, I realized the people working there were onto something. There was a clarity, serenity, and purpose in their eyes and in the way they moved and talked. This was a quality that most people I was surrounded by lacked in spades. I didn't quite know what it was, but I wanted and needed it badly.

And it was there that I was exposed to my first toolkit. However, this was no ordinary toolkit. It was a set of skills unlike any I'd been exposed to. This was a toolkit for the mind.

Up to that moment I'd never really thought of turning my attention inward. I'd never thought of looking at myself to see why I was unhappy, why I had so much mental anguish. I was too busy looking outward for someone or something to blame. But this turn inward was the orientation I was being invited to cultivate.

Mindfulness meditation, I discovered, is a skill that gives you the awareness to see, with focused clarity, what is happening in your mind and body. It gives you the ability to understand and work with all the thoughts and voices in your head. It helps you see what the real roots of suffering are and how to resolve the problems they cause. What I discovered was liberating — more effective than any pill, philosophy, or other supposed panacea. And it worked much better than raging against the machine.

So what was in that toolkit, you may ask, and why was it so helpful? In the initial training, I learned that to navigate life's inner and outer storms, you need two essential skills: awareness and compassion. They are like the wings of a bird, without which flight is impossible.

Awareness comes through practicing mindfulness, which is a way to cultivate attention and insight. Compassion allows you to meet yourself and life with kindness, care, and responsiveness. Having worked with people all over the world for twenty years, I have seen how important tenderhearted compassion is. There is so much pain in life. And it is sad to watch people needlessly add to that by beating themselves up. It is the love in our hearts that allows us to be vulnerable enough to recognize the burdens we carry. Love gives us a quiet strength that enables us to keep the critic at bay, hold our pain tenderly, and begin the journey of healing.

Even though I equipped myself with these wings, it is not as if I immediately took flight. As with anything in life, real change happened slowly. But those two qualities began to teach me how to turn the lens of attention toward myself, toward my own mind and heart, with kindness and clarity, which is not as easy as it sounds. As novelist Anne Lamott once wrote, "My mind remains a bad neighborhood that I try not to go into alone."

What did I discover when I started to look within? I saw how punishing I was with myself. I understood how cruel and savagely unforgiving I was about my own foibles and insecurities. I discovered how judgmental I was about everything I said and everything I did. And whenever I tried to do something new, I felt the unreasonable expectation to be perfect from the outset. Instead of appreciating the mess-ups and wrong turns, which are essential for learning, I would instead harshly chastise myself. All of this brought me to the realization that my inner critic was making my life miserable. If I continued listening to it, I would go on feeling hopeless, angry, unworthy, and depressed.

And so, as I took up the tools of awareness and compassion, I began the slow process of uprooting the critical voices within and the impossibly high standards they led me to set for myself. I started to be less influenced by the inner critic's attacks. I began to see not only that there was light at the end of the tunnel, but, more importantly, that there was a light being shined right in front of me by the brightness of my own awareness. Awareness would be the torch that lit my path to discovery and the key to cooling the fires that raged inside me. You too can free yourself from your inner critic. The tools and techniques described in this book will show you how.

How to Use This Book

You can approach this book as a map, a guide to exploring the jungles and thickets of the inner world, where your own inner critic resides. In this book you will discover what that critic is, how it manifests, where it comes from, and what strengthens and weakens it. This is a practical manual on how to skillfully and effectively work with it so it no longer causes you so much pain. The book is divided into five parts, as laid out below. Though you may wish to cherry-pick and go to the chapters that draw you most, you will likely get more benefit if you read the book sequentially.

Part 1: The Critic: The Big Picture

Part 1 explores the nature and prevalence of the inner critic and how it robs you of peace. This part also explains the critic's origin, function, and point of view.

The good news coming out of neuroscience is that your brain and your negative habits can change based on how you use your attention. This principle is known as neuroplasticity. The possibility of change through neuroplasticity underlies this book. In chapter 1 you will see how even long-held habits of self-judgment can be transformed by changing what you choose to focus on.

Chapter 2 looks at the prevalence of the judging mind in adults, children, and society in general, and demonstrates that you are not alone in your struggle with the inner critic. This harsh judge can be a tormentor, taskmaster, killjoy, and tyrant. As shown in this chapter, the critic can become a cause of depression and chronic low self-esteem if left unchecked.

Innumerable people, even successful CEOs and Ivy League professors, suffer from "imposter syndrome" — the feeling that they are a fraud. Chapter 3 describes this common phenomenon and the fears that go with it. This chapter shows how the critic feeds this sense of being a fake, and explains what you can do about it.

When you see how much your inner critic robs you of peace and self-esteem, you will be less apt to give it your loyalty and attention. Chapter 4 shows how the critic can stifle your joy in life, and includes case studies of what can happen when you let the critic take over.

Evolutionary biology reminds us that many of our thinking processes are hardwired, inherited from our family of origin and our culture. Chapter 5 explores the benefits of not condemning yourself for the way you got here and shows how you can move forward by understanding that so much is outside your control.

If the critic is so painful and seemingly dysfunctional, why do we have one, and what purpose does it serve? Chapter 6 answers these questions, explaining where the critic comes from, how it plays a role in your childhood development, and why it outstays its welcome.

Chapter 7 aims to help you understand the emotions and pain that lie beneath your inner critic's attacks. You will see how to identify what the critic is trying to say and why it is so concerned about your every move.

I often hear questions like "If I let go of my critic, how will I do my work? How will I get out of bed in the morning? What will motivate me to wash the dishes piling up in the sink or file my taxes?" Chapter 8 describes some common reasons for this sense of loyalty to the critic, and shows how people misattribute the qualities of discernment, evaluation, and conscience to the inner judge.

Part 2: Understanding Self-Judgment

Part 2 takes a closer look at what the critic does — what it says, how it says it, and how it knows exactly what to say to both get your attention and undermine your sense of well-being.

Chapter 9 reveals the more sinister consequences of what the critic does, and explains how self-judgments can attack your innate value, leading you to question your very worth as a person.

One of the main ways the critic operates is by attempting to persuade you that you are "not enough": not smart enough, not cute enough, not wealthy, healthy, or social enough. Chapter 10 explores this particular form of self-judgment and the impact it can have on your fundamental sense of well-being.

With the 20/20 hindsight you have after the fact, it's easy to give yourself a hard time about situations or decisions that didn't go as well as planned. Chapter 11 dissects this judging process, showing how it leads to regret and indecision, and how unnecessary and futile it really is.

The critic has many voices and comes in many guises.

Sometimes it appears as a coach or friend; other times, as a tyrant, perfectionist, or cajoler. These multiple voices can be likened to an "inner boardroom" that is always meeting to discuss and pass judgment on everything you do. Chapter 12 will help you identify the members of your inner boardroom.

Have you ever noticed how hard on themselves judgmental people can be? Chapter 13 examines this phenomenon and shows how the habit of judging others and the habit of judging yourself reinforce each other.

The critic's harsh words can impact you emotionally and physically, impinging on your energy level and mental clarity. Chapter 14 looks at all the ways the judging mind can affect you.

Chapter 15 deals with the ways your inner critic can influence your relationships. You will learn how judging others, particularly those close to you, can seriously undermine the health and well-being of your relationships.

Part 3: How to Work Mindfully with the Critic

In part 3 you will learn the skills essential for working with the critic. This part of the book will introduce you to a variety of methods for gaining the inner space to deal with self-judgment.

Chapter 16 delves into the life-transforming practice of mindfulness — what it is, what it does, and how it strengthens the muscle of self-awareness, which allows you to transform your relationship to the critic's judgments.

Despite their force, when you recognize judgments as simply thoughts, you begin to see that you have the power to influence them and not remain under their sway. In chapter 17 you will see how to bring the light of this awareness to your thinking.

Our judgments can be sticky, and our mind like Velcro, so that every judgment sticks hard and fast. Chapter 18 explains how to use nonidentification to make your mind more like Teflon so the judgments begin to roll off.

Chapter 19 discusses the insights you gain when you understand who and what the judge is, where it comes from, and what functions it serves. With that understanding, you can more easily separate yourself from it and its impact.

Chapter 20 considers the role of humor in dealing with the critic. The more you can find lightness in your relationship with the critic, the easier it is to deal with and the more joy you will find in life.

Often your (and your critic's) view of yourself and the world is distorted and heavily biased. By questioning that view, you can weaken the critic's hold over you. In chapter 21 you will learn how to challenge the perspective and basic assumptions of the judging mind.

Chapter 22 focuses on what happens when you've successfully implemented the strategies presented in this book and no longer care about the judgments the critic is hurling at you. When you adopt that mind-set, it doesn't matter whether the critic is operating or not because you've become immune to it.

Part 4: The Power of Love

There are many ways to work with negative forces of the mind. But love is the most powerful force at your disposal, and necessary in any deep work with the judging mind. Part 4 invites you into the domain of the heart.

In chapter 23 you will discover how to befriend yourself, including that scared, critical part of your mind that judges you. This work involves learning to be your own ally and biggest supporter.

Opening yourself to vulnerability is the first step in harnessing the power of love. Chapter 24 will introduce you to the vital role of vulnerability in dealing with the critic.

The transformative practice of kindness toward yourself is the subject of chapter 25. Self-kindness lays the groundwork for new neural pathways conducive to your treating yourself with respect and care.

Chapter 26 explains how compassion enables you to respond to your pain and self-judgment with kindness and care and how it helps you find strength, and establish healthy boundaries, in the face of harm.

In chapter 27 you will discover how to develop the powerful quality of self-forgiveness, which can release you from the tyranny of self-criticism for the ways you haven't acted perfectly in the past. With the support of self-forgiveness, you can move on with your life, without being bogged down by judgments from the past.

Part 5: Beyond the Critic

Part 5 concentrates on life beyond the critic, and the peace you can attain when you've put its negative impact behind you. In this part of the book, you will learn how to cultivate a sense of well-being for the rest of your life.

Paying attention to the good, which is covered in chapter 28, is one of the greatest antidotes to the critic. This is the opposite of the critic's negative slant and can help you develop a healthier, more positive orientation in life.

Chapter 29 explains how to take this brighter attitude and turn it toward others rather than seeing them through the critic's lens.

Chapter 30 describes how life looks and feels, and examines the horizons that open up, when you are no longer under the critic's wearisome spell.

Finally, chapter 31 reviews the key techniques for freeing yourself from self-judgment. Cultivating these skills, habits, and insights will help you live a more fulfilling life, one in which happiness and well-being are not just fleeting states, but your ongoing abode.

Resources: The Critic Toolbox reveals additional strategies for effectively disengaging from the critic's judgments and reducing their impact on your life. You can develop these skills in a very short time, but they are so helpful you can use them for a lifetime!

PART ONE

THE CRITIC:
THE BIG PICTURE

CHAPTER ONE

CHANGE IS POSSIBLE

◄ ►

Neuroplasticity and the Power of Choice

It's not what you say out of your mouth that determines your life, it's what you whisper to yourself that has the most power.

— ROBERT T. KIYOSAKI

When I first woke up to the fact that you can change your mind, I was blown away. And I don't just mean change your mind about a decision, but make a radical shift in how you think and feel. You can actually give your own mind a makeover.

I remember reading my journals from my late teens a while ago, and they read like a monologue of despair. I felt strangely sad and caring toward that teenager who was so lost in the negative swirls of his own mind. He did not know that change was possible; he felt lost in his negativity and cynicism. He was unaware that his pain would be the beginning of a search for answers, for tools and techniques that could lead him out of this pit of woe.

Luckily for him — for me — I stumbled on the pragmatic practice of mindfulness meditation. It seemed to offer a way out.

Not an easy or quick path, but nevertheless a way through the dangerous jungle of my inner world.

Mindfulness practice, though it has been around for thousands of years, has at its root a principle that has only recently been discovered by neuroscience — neuroplasticity, or the capacity of the brain to change and grow depending on what it pays attention to and how its attention is focused. This is the good news of human development: Our brain is not a fixed machine. On the contrary, it is dynamic, responsive, and capable of shifting, growing, and developing healthy habits that support happiness.

I didn't know back in those tormented teen years that I had a choice. That the programming I had inherited and learned was just that — programming. I hadn't yet realized that I could rewrite the code. That fact that I could hack my own brain turned out to be nothing short of a miracle.

What gives us that ability is mindfulness — the self-awareness that helps us understand the inner workings of our own minds, our programming. Mindfulness returns to us the power of choice, particularly when it comes to our mental habits and choices.

It was the practice of mindfulness that made me aware of the tyrannical self-judgments that were making my life miserable. I could see with a newfound perspective how hard I was on myself. I saw what impossibly high standards I had set for my life.

I also saw how this habit of faultfinding didn't just apply to me. I held everyone else under the same negative microscope. So, naturally, I was quite obnoxious to be around as a young man! I was idealistic, but with my mental sword I would slay everyone who didn't live up to my impossibly high standards and expectations. It was no fun, for me or for them. (I'm still apologizing to my family for putting them through that.)

So how did I change these patterns? For one thing, I realized that, due to their sheer number, the judgments flying my way were not about to stop anytime soon. Anyone who has tried meditating will know it is impossible to stem the tide of thoughts. But I saw that I didn't need to give them the attention they were demanding. And I certainly didn't need to believe them. I needed to heed the advice from a bumper sticker I often see in San Francisco today: "Don't believe everything you think."

I also realized that we can choose to focus our awareness on any number of things at a given moment. I realized that I didn't need to keep feeding the judgments with my attention. That I could turn my gaze elsewhere at my own bidding — to my body, or breath, or the beautiful blue sky, or the sounds of birds, or even traffic — and it felt liberating.

Neuroscience tells us that what we pay attention to can change the structure of the brain. Neuroscientist Donald Hebb's discovery in 1948 that neurons that fire together wire together has become a foundational scientific principle that allows for inner transformation. If I continue to give negative thoughts attention, then of course they grow in importance. If I stop giving them the time of day, then they have less room to take root and grow.

And if I focus not on what is wrong, but on what is good, positive, or possible, then my experience, affected by what I pay attention to, changes. Next time you are in a public place — a café, train station, or street — spend five minutes looking at everyone's faults and notice what you feel. It will probably not be a sense of joy and expansion. Then for the next five minutes try looking at everyone's goodness, strengths, and positive attributes. Doing that, you'll probably feel more connected, more positive, maybe even appreciative — I personally would much rather reside in that state.

So this is precisely what I decided to do. Thanks to the gift of awareness that was developing through mindfulness practice, I was able to give less attention to the tirades of my inner critic and the gloom it created. Instead I began to turn my awareness to what was working well, to what I was doing that was kind, effective, and successful. I started noticing what was uplifting, beautiful, and inspiring. This wasn't a denial of the negativity in the slipstream of my mind or the problems of the world. It was just a conscious decision to not be dragged into the gravitational pull of the judgments.

This isn't the only thing mindfulness allows you to do. Perhaps more important, once something is seen clearly with mindful awareness, it doesn't have the impact it did before. So as I began to recognize my judging thoughts clearly, it was as if I were seeing them in relief or projected onto a screen, and I could hold them at more of a distance and be less affected by them.

The other groundbreaking shift occurred when I took up the meditation of loving-kindness, which is a method of cultivating friendliness and unconditional care. This practice asks you to regard yourself with kindness, as you would a loved one, and offer loving words and genuine wishes of kindness to yourself. Through this technique, I learned to turn toward myself with love — which seemed a radical act for me at the time.

If you are reading this book, the idea of being kind to yourself is probably not a very familiar one. You may have already figured out that doing such a thing is not in the repertoire of the critic, which often regards us as unworthy of such kindness. In fact, it is the opposite of what the critic does, and this is why loving-kindness practice is such an effective method. This practice allows you to retrain your brain, creating new neural pathways conducive to self-kindness rather than self-hatred and self-condemnation.

When I first tried this, I found it almost impossible. It was like trying to melt an iceberg in my heart. But over time, with persistence and patience, that iceberg slowly began to melt, and I began to catch occasional glimpses of the possibility of being kind to myself, even forgiving myself and accepting all my foibles.

These two wings of a bird, awareness and kindness, allowed the step-by-step work I did with the inner voices that had up to then made my life challenging and painful. I began to see that change was possible and that if I could do it, anyone could.

⟢ PRACTICE ⟸
Looking on the Bright Side

Do this practice the next time you are in a public place. For the first five minutes, look around and focus on all the things you don't like, the things you think are wrong, bad, ugly. Look at the people around you and let your mind fixate on their faults or what could be improved upon. Notice what that negative, judgmental state of mind feels like.

Then for the following five minutes, notice all the things you like in the environment. Look at everything that is positive or uplifting or beautiful. At the same time observe the people around you and simply focus on what you like or appreciate in them, or on the positive attributes they possess. Again notice how you feel.

Can you see how shifting your attention to what is uplifting, good, and positive has a direct impact on your state of mind and heart?

Now do the same thing with yourself. Spend five to ten minutes thinking about all the things you like and appreciate about yourself. Reflect on your accomplishments, gifts, and positive qualities. Call to mind the kind or generous things you have done. Appreciate your body and all it does for you. Again notice how shifting your attention to what is good changes not only your mood, but also the way you feel about yourself.

Try to practice turning toward the positive in both yourself and others throughout your day, to train your mind's bias from the negative to the positive.

CHAPTER TWO

YOU ARE NOT ALONE

◄ ►

The Epidemic of Self-Judgment

I'm probably just as good a mother as the next repressed, obsessive-compulsive paranoiac.

— ANNE LAMOTT

Have you noticed how many people give themselves a hard time? How friends and colleagues routinely put themselves down and happily confess all their faults and problems? It is culturally acceptable to talk about your faults and challenges, and of course to complain ad nauseam about the faults of others. As Lucy so eloquently put it in a *Peanuts* cartoon (speaking to Charlie Brown): "The problem with you, Charlie, is that you are *you*."

At the same time it is quite the norm not to talk about one's successes, strengths, and accomplishments. In some cultures, that is considered gauche and egotistical. Being raised in England, I was taught it was a faux pas to speak of your talents and gifts or celebrate your victories. It is as if you are rubbing other people's nose in the dirt by doing so. Yet it is fine to lead with one's inadequacies and problems.

In the United States the mental health statistics are alarming. One in ten Americans is on some form of antidepressant. One in five took some kind of behavioral medication in 2010. The number of suicides is equally staggering: forty thousand per year. And that's just the numbers that are reported. Though the numbers may be higher in the United States than elsewhere, many industrialized countries report similarly alarming statistics.

Based on the work I have done with people over the past fifteen years on six continents, I believe the inner critic is a significant cause of much of the depression, anxiety, and suicide prevalent today. When the critic's voices are loud, sharp, and rampant, it is hard to keep a sense of self-worth or feel there is a meaning or purpose in life.

Though the statistics are startling, there is one sad but reassuring fact among them: you are *not* alone. One of the biggest burdens we can carry when we are depressed, or just lost in a swamp of self-reproach, is the troubling thought that we are unusual to have such problems. We mistakenly believe that we are the only ones afflicted by nagging, negative stories about ourselves. It is bad enough to have such troubling thoughts, but the idea that you may be the only "loser" in the room who has them is doubly shaming, and harder to work with.

In workshops that I lead about the inner critic, one of the most healing outcomes is people's realization that they are not the only ones with a judging mind. Isolation and the belief that you're the odd one out, that everyone but you is having a merry old time, just compounds these mental challenges.

When I have people pair up at an inner-critic workshop and share their list of self-judgments, there is at first a sense of great apprehension and embarrassment, and a fear of the shame that may ensue. But when they actually do share their lists, a collective relief sweeps the room. The realization that we share similar self-judgments and negative mental habits brings this sense of relief. The thought that we can help each other if we share a similar burden also nurtures an important sense of camaraderie and social support.

━━ PRACTICE ━━
Noticing the Critic Everywhere

As you go about your life — whether at home, at work, with friends, running errands, watching television — start paying attention to how you see the critic operating in other people. We can certainly observe it when hearing politicians and pundits barking on the radio or when movie critics are demolishing the latest film.

Also notice the inner critic in conversations, in the way people jokingly put themselves down: "Oh, you know me. I'm hopeless at math. Why don't you do the numbers?" "My hair looks terrible today." "I look awful in those photos." "I made a real mess of that meeting at work yesterday." These are all common parts of social conversation.

Observe what happens when you notice this behavior. Can you relate to others when they are putting themselves or others down? Does it feel familiar or even comfortable? Do you feel a sense of camaraderie? Can you see how ubiquitous this pattern is? Does it leave you feeling less alone, now that you can see you are not the only person with a sadistic inner voice? Similarly, do you feel compassion for others when they talk about themselves so negatively?

The more you can observe in this way, the more you will relieve yourself of the burdensome feeling that you are the only one with a problem, that you alone have a voice you should be ashamed of. Instead you may begin to feel a sense of connection with others, a feeling that you too are part of the shared human struggle, trying to find a way to be at peace amid all our conditioning and mental gyrations.

CHAPTER THREE

IMPOSTER SYNDROME

◄ ►

If They Really Knew Who I Am...

I have written eleven books but each time I think, "Uh oh, they're going to find out now. I've run a game on everybody and they're going to find me out."

— MAYA ANGELOU

A very common example of the ubiquitous nature of the critic is the phenomenon of "imposter syndrome" — the feeling that you don't deserve to be where you are in life. It's estimated that 70 percent of people have imposter syndrome. How many times have you been in front of a class, or asked to give a presentation as an authority on some issue, or invited to perform in a concert, or picked for the best sports team, and felt like a fake? Or what about those times when you have gone for an interview where you are supposed to present yourself as a specialist and felt like an imposter?

Imposter syndrome commonly appears as the voice that says, "Who do you think you are?" This voice of self-doubt and deprecation haunts multitudes. It even appeared to the Buddha on the night of his enlightenment. When I first heard that, I thought, "At least I'm in good company!" For a more contemporary example of how ubiquitous this pattern is, Meryl Streep, the most Academy Award–nominated actor in history, said in an interview, "Why would anyone want to see me again in a movie? And I don't know how to act anyway, so why am I doing this?"

Sometimes that feeling of fraudulence comes when you actually get the job. Have you ever felt that if people only knew who you really are, you'd be found out, they'd be disappointed, or you'd be fired on the spot? Whether you are a janitor or CEO, you're susceptible to this feeling of being a fraud.

Toward the end of his life, Einstein admitted that he felt like "an involuntary swindler." Almost every renowned figure has had their own version. "I am not a writer. I've been fooling myself and other people," John Steinbeck wrote in his diary in 1938. Facebook COO Sheryl Sandberg has said, "There are still days when I wake up feeling like a fraud." And, of course, if we listen to the whispers or taunts of the inner critic, we will firmly believe we ourselves are a fraud, that we don't deserve to be where we are.

People often get that feeling in relationships too. Perhaps you land the relationship or partner of your dreams. And as good as that is, you are plagued with a haunting feeling of anxiety that takes the form of "If they only knew what I am really like, they would leave." Such self-diminishment can actually jeopardize the very relationship we care about if we believe those thoughts.

For me there is nothing like being a mindfulness teacher to spark this sense of being an imposter. How often have I showed up to teach a class on meditation or given a lecture on patience, when one hour prior, I was sitting in traffic on the freeway, frustrated about the state of traffic and anxious about getting to my class on time? I was not looking like the picture of serenity many students would expect. I was not floating on clouds as I sat there inhaling exhaust fumes! Or I could be giving a lecture on how mindfulness helps develop a moment-to-moment attention and how that improves memory and spatial awareness. And yet, before going to that class, I had to spend fifteen minutes retracing my movements that day because I couldn't, for the life of me, find my keys!

Fortunately, I have learned enough about mindfulness to know it is not about being perfect, but about how you relate to and stay present for each moment's experience, with a kind, wise attention. And for me that sometimes means being present to anxiety, frustration, or confusion, just as it does for anybody else on the planet.

⟞ PRACTICE ⟝

Recognizing Imposter Syndrome

What if you were to believe you were the right person for the job or the perfect choice for your soul mate? How would it feel to stand at the front of an audience and know you had every right to be standing right there, with authority and confidence? Can you imagine taking your place in the boardroom and knowing you have every reason to be there?

It is possible to overcome imposter syndrome. Here's how:

STEP 1: Use mindful awareness to recognize imposter syndrome when it is operating. As soon as we see something with mindfulness, it can no longer hold us in its spell the same way it did when it was unconscious. Recognize imposter syndrome when it is operating. As soon as we are aware of something, it can no longer hold us in its grip the same way it did when it was unconscious. So although it can be painful to notice the pattern of imposter syndrome, doing so is the start of freeing yourself from its shackles.

STEP 2: Start to pay attention when those undermining thoughts are operating. Try to detect the voices that question your authority, experience, or ability. Notice what they are saying. It's only when we see those thoughts clearly that we can begin to distance ourselves from them and limit their impact.

STEP 3: Question the thoughts themselves. These thoughts don't have a monopoly on the truth, and the less we believe them, the more they will wither on the vine. We can begin to shift away from focusing on them or believing them, and instead focus on something that is more true, present, and positive.

STEP 4: Begin to remember your gifts, experience, and talent, which stand in direct opposition to the self-doubting thoughts. Since the critic is so pervasive, it's important to balance its taunts with an objective perspective. Instead of listening to all the reasons why you shouldn't be giving the presentation or getting the job, turn your attention to the unique set of strengths and skills you bring to any situation, person, or team. It's essential to keep doing this, to ground your perspective in reality, not some distorted view.

CHAPTER FOUR

THIEF OF PEACE

◄━ ━►

The Critic as the Cause of Low Self-Esteem

Stay out of the court of self-judgment, for there is no presumption of innocence.

— ROBERT BRAULT

How many times have you been enjoying a quiet Sunday afternoon, resting in your backyard in the late summer sun, perfectly at ease in the world, when suddenly a nagging voice pipes up and says something like, "Why are you wasting this perfectly good afternoon? You could be doing something more productive, like cutting the grass, clearing out all that clutter in the garage, or tending to those chores around the house that you said you would get to this weekend"? In a flash, that moment of tranquillity is gutted by a sense of guilt and anxiety.

It's the same when you go for an evening drive and realize the car has not been washed for months, the windows need to be cleaned, and the trash needs to be emptied. Then a voice rises up from the shadows and tells you why you don't deserve a nice car ride, but instead need to be reminded of how forgetful and lazy you are and why you need to get something done — anything, even something as simple as cleaning the car.

Likewise think about all the times you have gone to a dinner in your colleague's beautiful house, or visited your friend's idyllic children's birthday party, or taken a drive in your brother's new car, and instead of being able to enjoy the moment, you were side-tracked by the critic comparing your life to theirs, listing all the ways you don't measure up. Your inner judge implies you are a lesser person because your cooking is not up to snuff, your house is too scruffy to host a party, your children's birthday parties are disorganized, and your car is an embarrassment.

That voice of judgment seems ready, at a moment's notice, to kill the joy of the moment and remind us that we don't deserve to have fun or relax, aren't worthy of taking care of ourselves, aren't good enough in comparison to others, and that if we only listened and obeyed the critic's commands, we would be a better, happier, and more successful person. What may start as an innocuous voice builds up steam over time until it becomes the loudest thing in your head and an incessant rumination, like a yapping dog constantly snapping at the heels of your goodness.

If we listen to all those disparaging remarks, what happens? We shift from enjoying the present moment to feeling unworthy, unhappy, and deficient. In my experience in working with thousands of people over the past two decades, I have seen time and again how people fall victim to their inner critic and its harsh words. The sad consequences of taking in all its sharp judgments are a dampening of joy, a reduction in well-being, a lowering of self-esteem, and greater chances of depression and anxiety. The net result is a low-grade feeling of shame.

I once worked with a delightful man in his sixties named James who had been unable to get out from under the oppression of his inner critic. He looked gray and weather-beaten and talked about feeling smothered, as if under a cloud of shame. He was unable to distinguish his own thoughts from the noise of the critic, so he was plagued by an ongoing tirade of judgment in his head.

I felt terribly sad for him. He couldn't see that he was a good person, trying to do his best, who genuinely cared about his colleagues, his family, and people in general. I could sense a sparkle as he talked about his love of nature and animals. Yet his whole being was shrouded, as though under a heavy cloak. Despite the brief joys he could find in his life, the experience of his critic constantly reminding him that he was not good enough, that he was a failure, made it hard for him to find any peace of mind.

If the critic were a person dishing up those endless tirades, we would call it emotional or psychological abuse and perhaps seek some kind of intervention, tell them to go away, or get a restraining order. But because the criticism takes place within the quiet confines of our own head, it goes unnoticed by others; it becomes like our own living-room furniture — background and familiar — and so goes unchallenged.

I remember a similar situation: I was coaching a woman who worked as a top medical researcher in New York. In her late thirties, she was quite accomplished and had consulted on national health policy issues on Capitol Hill in Washington, DC. Yet her self-assessment was very negative. All she could fixate on and use to evaluate herself was her inability to have successful long-term relationships. Sadly, she was unable to enjoy and celebrate the achievements of her illustrious career.

This particular challenge in her personal romantic world was the only lens she could look through to see whether she was a worthy person. As a consequence, she felt depressed and hopeless, blind to her innate gifts, strengths, and talents. She was looking at herself through a distorted lens. No wonder she felt miserable.

The more we listen to the negative, distorted inner voices of self-judgment that directly attack our self-worth, the more likely we will be to have an imbalanced sense of ourselves. We will be prone to disconnecting from a sense of our innate value and therefore have a tendency to feel despondent about ourselves. Failing to feel that sense of innate goodness at the heart of who we are means we lack a strong foundation on which to build a happy, flourishing life.

➤ PRACTICE ➤

Correcting the Inner Balance Sheet

The inner critic is like a bad accountant who only looks at the column in red, or the liabilities, without taking the assets into consideration. To practice getting a clearer view of your internal balance sheet, try taking a whole day where you notice the positive aspects of yourself:

- Pay attention to your unique gifts, skills, and qualities.
- Notice when you act in positive, kind, caring ways.
- Observe the moments of quiet joy and ease.
- Take in any moments of appreciating what you are wearing or how you look.
- Acknowledge when you talk to people with politeness, respect, or interest.
- Look for any positive impact you are bringing to a situation, person, or environment.
- Take in those times when you are spontaneously generous to others.
- Notice your sense of humor and your capacity to enjoy life.

Sometimes when we do this, it can turn up the volume of our critic. The critic may ridicule any attempt to look on the bright side of things. See if you can begin to correct the balance sheet by shifting your perspective in the following ways:

- When people compliment you, take a moment to take it in rather than dismissing it or questioning their motives.
- When someone sends you an email thanking you for something you did or said, take it in and notice how it feels.
- When you feel you did a good job at some task at work, at home, or taking care of your family, also let that in.

The more you can acknowledge the goodness of an action, the more you will realize it comes from your innate goodness — your authentic nature.

CHAPTER FIVE

YOU ARE NOT YOUR FAULT

◄ ►

Not Taking Your Thoughts Personally

Before you go and criticize the younger generation, just remember who raised them.

— ANONYMOUS

There are a few times in life when a certain word or phrase catches you off guard, and it resonates with you so much that it penetrates into the deepest recesses of your being. That was what happened when I heard the statement "You are not your fault" from my friend and fellow meditation teacher Wes Nisker.

Somehow, when I heard that, a whole layer of burden melted, as though I were taking off a backpack filled with heavy stones. I suddenly realized I no longer needed to drag around the dead weight of believing that who or how I was, was all my fault.

"I am not my fault — what a concept," I mused. "What a different way to see myself." I, like most people, had been carrying around the notion that I *was* my fault. That I was the person to blame for being disorganized, being sensitive, and having low energy, and for all the other things that, according to the critic, were wrong with me.

I wondered what it would be like not to take all of that so personally. Not to put the blame or responsibility on myself. That, of course, didn't mean abdicating personal responsibility for how I behave or act now. It just meant not blaming myself for all my idiosyncrasies, deficiencies, and foibles. It meant letting myself off the hook for the cultural, social, biological, and familial conditioning that was instilled at an early age and has had a huge impact on who I am now.

Think about how this is true for you — how you are also not your fault. Did you ask for this particular body shape, color, or size? Did you request this particular obsessive, controlling mind? Did you order your ethnicity? Did you select your emotional style — which might tend toward the histrionic, irrational, or volatile — from a catalog? Did you ask for the dysfunctional family that left you with emotional scars and neuroses? Probably not.

There is a strand of New Age thinking that says we did ask for exactly what we get in this lifetime. Whether it be our body, our family, or our trauma and life challenges. I strongly challenge this notion. Where is the empirical proof that this is so? There may be many "past life" psychics and theorists who claim you came in asking for all this. However, that's a speculative belief system that cannot be proved. More than that, it leaves people feeling guilty for their difficult and often painful circumstances.

In reality, we are the sum of innumerable causes and conditions that are impossible to trace. Who we are and how we end up depend on a multitude of circumstances outside our control. Just think about the simple fact of where you were born and how that shaped and influenced you. How different would you be had you been born to an Inuit tribe in Northern Canada in freezing temperatures, or to textile merchants in a city in Ghana, or to tango teachers in Buenos Aires?

Think about the difference it would have made if your IQ were 70 points higher. Or if you had (or didn't have) a learning difficulty when you were a child. Or your parents separated (or didn't separate) when you were young. Or you just happened to be good at chess and became a national chess champion. Or the town you lived in was wiped out by a tornado. So many factors, so many influences, that go into shaping us are beyond our control.

Yet somewhere along the line, we took responsibility for all of it. The ego in all its hubris stood up one day and said, "Yes, the buck stops here — it is all my fault. I am the sole determining factor that makes me who and what I am. Nothing else matters. I succeed or fail, make or break it, depending on what I do."

Take a moment to see the big picture of how you got to be here at all, on this floating ball of rock spinning across the universe, and the innumerable factors that influence you socially, personally, and genetically. Looking at the broader picture can allow compassion to arise for whatever challenges and peculiar traits, habits, and foibles you have inherited or developed. Why? Because it gets you to see that you are not your fault, that you simply get dealt a hand when you step into this life, a bit like betting blind on a hand in a Texas Hold 'em poker game.

Of course, how we play with the cards we are dealt, once we grow up and become adults, becomes much more of our responsibility. But even then, we can't underestimate how many of our responses to those same cards of life are affected by influences that are somewhat arbitrary and out of our control.

There's a saying that goes, "It's not what you came in with that makes a difference, but how you work with it." Or to paraphrase psychologist Carl Jung, "I am not what happened to me. I am what I choose to become." Our job is not to chastise and

apportion blame for who and what we are. Our work is simply
to meet ourselves with a kind, inquisitive attitude and respond to
the raw material of what we have to work with in this life. This
is a very different orientation from the attitude of the judge that
blames and rejects. This orientation allows us to meet ourselves
with acceptance and offers more room for our weird and wonderful and sometimes dysfunctional ways.

In a similar way your mind or your critic is not your fault.
Nor are the innumerable judging thoughts that your mind comes
up with. You don't have to take any or all of it so personally. The
critic's judgments are not actually who you are. The critic, like
everything else, is a result of conditioning, a necessary part of
childhood development. (We will explore this theme in greater
depth in chapter 6.) The fact that the critic may have outlived its
welcome or use is, again, not your fault. But what you do need to
do now is take responsibility for the judgmental voices that have
taken up residence in your mind, and ask them to leave if necessary — or at least not invite them to stay for dinner!

As with judgments, so it is with thoughts. You are not your
thoughts. There is no "one" behind your thoughts. Thoughts
think themselves. The brain thinks up to sixty to seventy thousand
thoughts a day. That is a lot of thoughts! How many of them did
you actually think deliberately? More likely, they just sprouted
like mushrooms in a damp forest.

When you can take a step back with awareness and look at
this whole sideshow of thoughts without being so entangled in
them, you can sense the possibility of space and freedom. Not
only can you release responsibility for the thoughts in your head,
but with mindful awareness you can begin to distance yourself
from their meaning and impact too. Then they won't hit you in
the same painful way because you are not taking them to be the

voice of truth, but simply thoughts coming and going like bubbles in a spring.

⟶ PRACTICE ⟵
Not Taking It Personally

On a sheet of paper list in one column all the things you blame yourself for or think are your fault. Then next to each item, in a separate column, make a note about whether you are actually, realistically to blame for that item.

For example, you might write in the first column that you are overweight compared to the average. In the next column you would write some of the causes and conditions contributing to your weight that are outside your control and not your fault — for example: obesity runs in your family; or you have type 2 diabetes; or you have a very slow metabolism; or you were born with a larger-than-normal build.

Again, this is not about shirking personal responsibility, but about seeing the larger causes and conditions that influence your life. This can help counteract the critic when it isolates specific things about you and accuses you of being at fault.

Another example: In the first column you might write that you are socially timid, which your inner critic views as a problem and your fault. In the second column you might note that you grew up in an area where your family was part of a religious, social, or ethnic minority and where you were bullied, rejected, or scorned for being different. Years of such treatment were thus in part perhaps responsible for your feeling a completely natural sense of fear or caution in social situations.

Once you have finished both columns, take some time

to reflect, and notice how it feels to look at your life from a big-picture perspective. Rather than look at the issue or behavior or characteristic in isolation, see how it came about — through numerous causes and conditions that were far outside your control. Once you see such things more objectively, you can peel off the layer of shame and embarrassment. Ironically, that frees up energy for you to respond to these things with more clarity and responsibility, and actually helps you take effective action if necessary.

CHAPTER SIX

HOW DID I GET HERE?

⸺ ▶ ◀ ⸺

The Origin and Function of the Critic

Don't wait for the Last Judgment. It happens every day.

— ALBERT CAMUS

In a meditation course a lawyer once referred to the critic as a bad roommate who is always criticizing you for not doing anything right. A lot of people were nodding their heads in agreement as he spoke. During that course "the unpleasant roommate" became a synonym for all the unhealthy voices in our head.

Later someone noted that the critic wouldn't be so bad if it were only one roommate living in her head. But, she said, it's more like having a whole college dorm in your mind! She commented that "there are so many critics in there, and they are all making a racket, even in the middle of the night!" I had to agree, and added that it's not a party I want to be invited to. But the critic doesn't care about invitations. It just barges in, often at the most inappropriate moment.

If the critic is such an unwanted guest, why are so many people plagued by it? Nature rarely, if ever, makes anything that does not serve a purpose. So what is the purpose of the critic, and how did it get there?

There are many psychological explanations for the presence of the critic. Freud, one of the founding fathers of psychology, referred to it as the "super-ego." For him the super-ego was an essential component of the psyche whose task was to rein in the impulses of the "id." The id is the more primal, unconscious, sexual forces that lie within us. If these were not contained, he posited, it would lead to a rampant acting out of these aggressive, self-centered forces, which would make living in a civil society almost impossible. (The movie *Lord of the Flies* portrays this kind of reality, with its harrowing consequences.)

To put it in nontechnical terms, infants and children need to maintain the maximum flow of love, affection, and care from their caregivers, not only for survival, but for optimal development. This is partly why babies are born so adorably cute that we want to love and take care of them. In order to fit into the particular family system and norms you found yourself in as a child, you needed some faculty that would allow you to control the more wayward forces of anger, rage, greed, and selfishness that were running through darling little you.

Given that those forces are so strong, you needed an equally powerful mechanism to curb them. And there's hardly a greater weapon than shame to shut down a strong force in ourselves. Just think about the ways you were shamed as you were growing up, as a prompt to curb those urges.

In one of many fierce fights with my older brother, I once called him a "bloody liar" after protesting to my parents that he was lying about some prank we had gotten in trouble for. My father, who was Catholic and furious on hearing me utter a profanity, proceeded to — literally — wash my mouth out with soap and water, claiming that swearing was sinful.

As you can imagine, I learned pretty quickly that it was not okay to swear, that I would be punished and shamed for doing so. So in order to preempt any future humiliation, my critic was very quick to remind me that swearing was bad, wrong, and shameful, and especially not to be done around my family.

In a way the critic was doing its job, trying to protect me from further public embarrassment and familial rejection. The problem is that it does not go away. It's like a broken record, constantly repeating. It keeps harping on as if transgressing like that again will have dire consequences, even decades after the actual incident, which of course is rarely true.

My father lives five thousand miles away and probably swears more than I do. Yet even today if I swear in public, I can feel a twinge of guilt and an unconscious concern that some judge's hammer will come down and rule against me.

The critic learns to anticipate the judgments and condemnation of others — particularly our parents, religious leaders, teachers, influential friends, relatives, and other authority figures. In order to protect us from being rejected or shamed by them, the critic learns to internalize their rules.

To see this in action, just observe young boys and girls playing and notice the various rules they have learned and strictly apply to each other. Mostly they are just repeating the many rules and cultural norms they have been taught at home or in school. Simple, right-and-wrong codes of conduct. And if you violate the code, you will be punished, or at least banished from the group or game.

Look at how, even today, boys are taunted by peers and adults with shaming comments for any expression of softness or vulnerability, in order to keep them firmly in a stereotypical masculine, if not macho, mold. They can be labeled weak, soft, or a pushover if they display "feminine" attributes. These young males then repeat what they have been told and internalized, and pass it on to their peers, and eventually to their own children. So the cycle of shaming continues from generation to generation.

Girls are not exempt from this social judgment and shaming. In fact it may be more intense for them. How often are girls told that it's unladylike and unfeminine to be aggressive or assertive, and that they should instead be kind and supportive? Sheryl Sandberg, COO of Facebook, in her book *Lean In*, observes that when girls display natural leadership skills at a young age, they are often labeled as bossy, to shame them into a more socially acceptable, traditional female role of deference.

The power of this need to conform is perhaps most evident during the teenage years, when it is considered essential to fit in and be accepted by one's peers. And this is an age where the inner critic becomes more vocal, more evident on the surface, and at times intensely cruel and shaming. Teen suicide is one of the extreme consequences of this crushing humiliation and punishment from the critic.

One important point to note is that the critic is not a particularly sophisticated mechanism, partly because it is almost fully developed by age eight. It operates with a child's perspective and voice. This is why it has a simplistic outlook and a rigid code of good and bad, right and wrong. This explains, in part, why reasoning with the critic tends to go nowhere — the critic is inflexible in its thinking and incapable of grasping ambiguity and subtlety.

By the time you're an adult, the critic has long outlived its usefulness. When you were young, it was an essential tool that your psyche employed to help you fit in and optimize the flow of affection. But over time it develops into the voice of your conscience, the authority on what is good or bad, and can heavily influence your choices. Even worse, it has the hubris to think it can decide whether you are worthy of love or are a good person at all.

Some argue that the inner critic emerges out of an innate negativity bias that has its roots in survival. In terms of evolution the ability to notice what is wrong, problematic, or potentially challenging helps us survive by enabling us to predict and prepare for the worst and anticipate potentially life-threatening situations in our environment. However, when that skill is turned on ourselves, it is not necessarily so helpful. Ironically, when this negativity bias diminishes our own worth, we tend to function less well. This puts us in a worse position to survive both inner and outer challenges, and it hinders our ability to flourish.

This is why, in dealing with the critic, you need to bring a lot of discernment and wisdom to bear. This involves acknowledging the critic's value and role in your past but, at the same time, intercepting it when it is not helpful or relevant in the present.

PRACTICE

Understanding the Origin of the Critic

In a journal or in a quiet meditation, take some time to ponder the origins of your inner critic. What brought it into being? What triggered it? Think about whether your judge has the voice or tone of authority figures from your past. Reflect on the following questions:

- Do your judgments sound like your mother's or father's voice?
- Do the critical thoughts have a religious overtone to them, perhaps internalized while growing up in a faith that had strong views of right and wrong?

- Were you teased by siblings who had strong views about you that were not kind?
- Were you raised by a grandparent or nanny who had their own strong opinions about who you should be and what was right and proper?
- In your teenage years were you particularly affected by your peers and their harsh rules and judgments?
- Did your judgments form as you internalized the way your family or caregivers were harsh, critical, and rejecting of themselves or others, and did you learn to mirror that behavior when relating to yourself?
- How might your judging mind initially have developed to help you fit into the particular family structure and culture you grew up in? Perhaps it was to dampen impulses, energies, and reactivity that could have caused you to be rejected or reprimanded by your caregivers. Or it could have been simply to repress emotions that were not welcome in the family, like sadness or anger.

Since we are social creatures, our need for love and affection are paramount, and the critic, at least initially, helped keep you in harmony with that flow of connection. For this reason we don't need to judge the judge. We can have compassion for the pain from which it arose, from a deep need to be loved and cared for. And, at the same time, we can recognize why the critic is so strong — it developed at an early age, for self-protection, and laid down neural pathways that were only strengthened as the years went by.

CHAPTER SEVEN

IN THE CRITIC'S DEFENSE

◄ ►

Understanding the Critic's Point of View

Write how you want, the critic shall show the world you could have written better.

— OLIVER GOLDSMITH

As miserable as the critic can make you feel, what if the critic is right? What if you need it in order to function, survive, and avoid the risk of humiliation and loss of love? What if, underneath its cold, harsh judgments, there are grains of deep truth that we need to heed?

Some schools of thought do take a kinder view of the critic. Internal family systems is a psychotherapy modality that encourages people to understand the various voices and subpersonalities that exist within their minds, including the critic, the manager, exiled parts, and so on. This form of therapy is based on the premise that once we identify and work with the needs, fears, and perspectives of the subpersonalities, as well as the emotion and history underlying them, we can find more skillful ways to relate to, understand, and integrate them. So then we can find a different way to relate to the critic, one that is not destructive, but that allows an inclusive and constructive dialogue with this voice and its perspective.

Similarly, Voice Dialogue, another psychotherapeutic modality, recognizes that our mind comprises numerous voices, or subpersonalities. From this perspective, the critic is simply trying to help us but is a misguided, sometimes harmful ally whose message has become distorted. We need to work with it patiently, to engage it in conversation and understand its point of view and reasoning.

Such psychotherapeutic orientations encourage us to seek the grain of truth in the critic's words, discerning what is useful in its message and sensing the fear or vulnerability the critic is trying to protect. These schools of psychology infer that the critic is attempting to help or protect us, but in a distorted, dysfunctional way, and that it can be transformed into a helpful ally if we reason with it, using clarity and understanding.

There is much validity to these perspectives. The critic, at an early age, was the voice that figured out all the ways we could be vulnerable, get hurt, and be shouted at, ridiculed, or rejected. That part of our ego was trying its best to make sense of the rules of our family, colleagues, friends, religion, and school so we could fit in, be liked, and not lose favor or, worse, lose love and affection. The critic quickly taught us what to do or not to do in order to survive. This was absolutely necessary.

The problem is that the mechanism of the critic does not know how or where to stop. It's basically lived past its sell-by date. Once you figure out how to navigate basic societal rules and norms and are old enough to take care of yourself, you no longer need that harsh voice haranguing you at every turn. You can then employ more reason, reflection, and compassion to navigate the challenges of living.

At some point it is no longer life or death if someone does not like what you said or did, or gets angry at you for expressing strong emotions. You can handle those things in a way that may have been scarier when you were young and totally dependent on others for survival. As you grow older, you no longer need to abide by the same strict rules that were necessary to follow in order to survive as a child.

But, unfortunately, the critic lacks the wisdom to understand this. The neural pathways of judgment are so ingrained they become second nature. They just keep trucking along. In fact, judgments often pick up steam as we get older. And as neuroplasticity suggests, the more we listen to the judge, the deeper its roots take hold — the more we heed it, the more we feed it. We become what we practice. So if we have made a lifetime habit of giving credence and attributing authority to the critic, it will have a lot of power over us.

Listening to the critic's point of view to extract useful information is a bit like trying to extract new information from a broken record. If someone is basically saying the same thing in ten different ways, there may not be much value in hearing the content yet one more time.

Nevertheless the critic can be a rich mine to probe for answers about the origins of certain thoughts, views, judgments, and reactions. A useful line of inquiry when any judgment is happening is to ask, "What is really going on here?" It is important to ascertain the actual data. What are the facts of the situation? It is also then helpful to probe for what may be going on at a deeper level. What might the critic be reacting to and trying misguidedly to defend against or attack?

As an example, some years ago I was driving my car, minding my own business, riding over the Golden Gate Bridge. Instead of enjoying the breathtaking view of the skyline of San Francisco, I was listening to my critic harping on about how I don't take care of business well enough and how I'm always dragging my heels. As the judge goes on, I ask myself: "What is going on here? Where did this come from? Why is my critic so up in arms and interfering with this gorgeous drive?"

And then I get it. I see my "check engine" light is still on, which reminds me I haven't changed the oil and am a month late on that. I also see that I did not replace my rear wiper blade, which is now carving a nice curved skate mark on the back window — that alone could be enough to warrant the judge's commentary.

But I'm also aware that I'm going to the airport to pick up my new business associate, who is very efficient, loves cars, and maintains his BMW immaculately. I'm suddenly caught in the grip of comparison. I want my associate to think well of me, particularly since we are going into a business venture together, and I'm concerned he will notice the state of my car and regard my lack of attention to automotive details as symbolic of someone who does not follow through on things.

The old warning signals are going off unconsciously, and my judge is admonishing me in the hope that its chastising will get me to actually take action, bring this procrastination on car maintenance to an end, and at the same time look more reliable.

What the critic does not understand is that its conclusions are not necessarily logical. My irrational fears about what the state of my car means to my colleague may be just that — irrational fears. Most likely, he will not notice or care about my engine light or windshield wiper.

The second and perhaps more important thing about the critic in this connection is that its wrathful attacks leave me feeling bad about myself and a little stupid. This is triggered by the reflection that it is not rocket science to get your oil changed. I notice this leads to a slight sense of being overwhelmed at all the other things that are left untended to in my busy life. Yet these thoughts and feelings are hardly good motivators for taking swift action to maintain my car. Their net effect is more likely to be a sense of hopelessness about myself because, according to the critic, I cannot take care of even simple things. This leaves me with a feeling of inertia and a sense of wanting to give up — the kind of sentiments expressed by the phrase "Why bother?"

Now my deeper sense of inadequacy — that I'm not together enough to take care of things — has been pointed out and verified with evidence. Even if I do fix the car, it doesn't matter, as my real nature, according to the critic, has been shown to be flawed. What is perhaps a well-intentioned critique (not wanting me to lose my colleague's respect) becomes a judgment about my worth as a person, which then stifles any positive, forward-moving energy.

As you can see, this is a lose-lose proposition. You could say the critic ends up as victor in the game of who is right, who shouts loudest. But it is only right if I give it that power and lofty position of authority. And, of course, that victory proves to be hollow if the very thing the critic is trying to protect, which is me, feels even less happy or motivated than prior to its attacks.

Clearly, we need a different strategy. It is important to discover what fears, vulnerabilities, and other emotions are driving the critic so that we fully understand what lies behind its judgments. Only then can we develop effective strategies to deflect its attacks, work with it skillfully, and begin to live with a greater sense of independence and well-being.

⫟ PRACTICE ⫞

Unearthing the Truth

In this practice you are going to be like a social archaeologist, digging for the causes underlying a particular judgment. This requires some journaling and reflection. You will be writing in two columns. In the first column write out one of your more common self-judgments. In the second column reflect on what lies behind this particular criticism. Do this for several of the criticisms you most often hear from your critic.

For example, you may have a voice that says, "You are never going to get your life together." Write that statement in the first column. Now reflect on what may be underlying such a scathing put-down of your potential. In the second column write what you think might be behind this judgment. Perhaps it is fear about not getting your career together in the way you would like. Perhaps the judgment comes from comparing yourself to your siblings, who happen to be more successful and thriving. Maybe you have doubts stemming from times in the past when you lacked organization or drive.

Sometimes the critic's voice is just a repetition of a statement hurled at you in moments when your parents were exasperated with the difficulty you had in preparing for exams at school. Or maybe you look at your parents and feel they didn't get their own lives together, and you have anxiety about that happening to you.

Digging deeper, you may uncover further layers of vulnerability. Perhaps you are in your forties or fifties, and you are concerned that if you don't get things more together, you will be struggling financially in your later years, and you worry about who will take care of you.

Sometimes the judging voice is just an old habit, a knee-jerk response. Like when you open a closet door and see piles of old clothes, books, and boxes that have yet to be organized and your automatic response is to chastise yourself for not getting it together. Or maybe that cluttered closet triggers thoughts of all the other parts of your life you feel need more organization and attention. Then you quickly feel overwhelmed, and that's where the judgment springs from, as a defense against the flood of emotion.

And last but not least, listen for any grain of truth about the actual situation. Perhaps the critic's statement reflects a genuine aspiration to be more organized. It may also imply a real need for taking some concrete steps to help yourself get more organized, which could require getting support or dedicating more time to the issue.

Once you have written out some judgments and their possible causes, notice whether that helps you understand the situation more fully. Does seeing the bigger picture take some of the sting out of the critic's attack or give you more ways to intervene in the cycle of criticism or to address what it is pointing to? Most importantly, does it allow you to see yourself with more compassion than judgment, now that you better understand the origins of the critic's harsh words?

CHAPTER EIGHT

FROM JUDGMENT TO DISCERNMENT

⇐ ⇒

Mistaken Loyalty to the Critic

I have yet to find the man, however exalted his station, who did not do better work and put forth greater effort under a spirit of approval than under a spirit of criticism.

— CHARLES SCHWAB

Have you ever had the feeling that without the judge rattling around in your head, you would never get out of bed in the morning, rarely clean your house, and probably not bother doing any work or even take a shower? I have heard a similar story countless times. Many people feel that if they didn't follow the admonitions of the critic, they would end up lazy, good-for-nothing slobs.

Their argument assumes that if they were not under the influence of the critic, nothing would get done, that they need the critic's barking voice to get them out the door or motivate them to function. My advice to them is that there are far more kind, considerate, and inspiring ways to motivate ourselves than the bullwhip or the shaming stick. Numerous management studies show that people are far more motivated and engaged when inspired by a leader who is encouraging, positive, and focused on what is possible rather than on faults and foibles. What we need is to stay connected with what gives us meaning, purpose, and value. We need to orient ourselves toward all that is possible rather than fixate on the critic's negative scenarios.

Those same people may say they would be unable to make wise, informed decisions or ethical choices without the judge informing them of what is right and wrong. Likewise, a bright lawyer I work with who made his way to partner in his law firm in a short time quips that without his critic and its sharp-pointed judgments, he'd be sunk, outdone by all the other sharp, judging attorneys.

Let us tackle these issues separately, starting with ethical choices. As discussed earlier, the critic is a crude mental mechanism that has a pretty simplistic view of the world and of what is right and wrong. It's about as sophisticated as the eight-year-old brain that developed it.

What is important to remember is that we all have a more sophisticated way of navigating ethical dilemmas than relying on the simplistic views and advice of our critic. We all have a conscience, a moral compass, that we can listen to and that is not as narrow in its thinking as our judgmental mind.

At times, we can trust our heart to tell us what feels kind and fair, and what feels mean, selfish, or cruel. At other times we can listen to our gut, to our intuition, for similar guidance. We can also navigate ethical concerns through reasoning — by understanding that actions have consequences and acting in a way that takes into account the impact of our behavior on others. We can also use our empathy skills, putting ourselves in another's shoes and using as a reference point the principle that we should treat others the way we'd like to be treated.

When we unhook from the grip of the judge's simplistic and moralistic positions, we can inquire into why we act in ways that aren't always the most skillful or helpful. For example, I worked with a client, a Scottish woman in her midthirties, happily married yet driven to have affairs with older men. She felt terribly ashamed for this acting out and yet felt unable to stop it. Not only did she feel powerless to restrain herself and fear wrecking her marriage, but her judge was viciously attacking her, writing her off as a bad, unworthy, immoral person.

This kind of inner aggression kills the spirit of inquiry as to why we are doing such painful things to ourselves and others. When she was able to create space between herself and her critic's tirades, she was able to inquire into what was prompting her to seek love or affection outside her marriage.

She began to see how she projected her own negative view of herself onto her partner, assuming that he also harbored the same harsh, judgmental feelings toward her. Unable to talk about it with him, she stayed stuck in a spiraling negative view of herself. That descent into self-hate kept prompting her to seek more approval from others outside her relationship. That hunger for attention and affirmation exerted enough inner pressure to make her sexually act out, against her better judgment.

We always have the power to break these cycles. But the critic, contrary to its own claim that it helps us navigate these realms, simply makes us feel worse and stops the stream of inquiry and understanding necessary to bring the unhealthy pattern to an end.

Another way we are loyal to the critic is believing that without its sharp judgments we would not be at our best in our work. After all, in many professions — from emergency room nurse, to police officer, to Wall Street trader — success requires a critical faculty. People often say their work depends on making fast judgments and that without the critic they would be left behind by their peers.

What is key in working with the critic is to learn to differentiate between discernment (a necessary tool) and negative judgment (an unhealthy habit). By ignoring the critic we are not throwing out our capacity to evaluate. On the contrary, we are enhancing that capacity. Discernment is clearer and leaves some room for a greater perspective, whereas judgment (in the sense we are referring to in this book) is reactive and closed-minded. The judge adds a value-laden quality to our perception. That is often unnecessary and, when it is about ourselves, implies an attack on our value as a human being.

Take, for example, your exercise regimen. As we all know, it is easy to have good intentions, particularly in regard to an enthusiastic New Year's resolution to get in better physical shape. Yet it is easy for such noble aspirations to fall by the wayside come mid-March or even February, and the gym can quickly become a distant memory.

From an objective standpoint, if you have indeed stopped working out, and you are putting on weight and feel more sluggish, it is not difficult to conclude that your exercise regimen is not working. That is the raw data that you can easily observe. The judge, on the other hand, not only notices the data, but also makes a value-laden judgment that attacks your worth — you are lazy, a slob, you'll never get yourself or your body together, and so on.

It is clear in this case that you don't need the additional comments of the judge to evaluate the effectiveness of your exercise program. In fact, its abusive snipes about your latest athletic failure will probably lead you to feel more hopeless, making it even less likely you'll get yourself to the gym. Your judge is quick to remind you of all the previous resolutions that have not borne fruit. "So why bother starting in the first place?" it says, as if offering kind or sage advice. In the end it's as if you've failed before even starting.

The difference between discernment and judgment shows up socially as well. All too often we are swept up in critical judgments about others, looking through the crude lens of the critic. When evaluating others, how quickly can we fall into writing someone off for their political views, the way they dress, their lifestyle choices, or the way they raise their children? This is not just an evaluation of a particular thing that they do, but a judgment about them as a person. The judging mind can be quick to dismiss others for the smallest thing. And, of course, the more we do that to others, the more we do it to ourselves. We need to ask ourselves, "Is this a habit I want to strengthen?"

The workplace is also an important place to observe this distinction between judgment and discernment, especially if you manage people and need to discern their strengths and the areas where they need to grow. If you have worked for a harsh boss, you know their judgments are hardly the ones that get you to perform well. Motivating people with fear or shame has never been a good long-term plan for employee engagement, retention, or creativity! A truly effective leader is one with emotional intelligence, who can discern the strengths and areas of lack in their team, and support the growth of others not by shaming or judging, but through feedback, encouragement, and constructive criticism.

And, as always, we can apply that lesson to ourselves. We can learn to discern rather than judge. We can look at our messy garage and simply discern that it requires sorting or needs a thorough cleaning, rather than getting on our own case for being disorganized. If our car is dirty, we don't need to make it mean something about our value as a person. It may just mean that we don't care so much about our car and how it looks, that we see the car as just something to get around in, or that we are simply too busy and have other priorities.

━ PRACTICE ━

Replacing Judgment with Discernment

Identify a few of the practical things or organizational tasks in your life that are problematic or need your attention. It could be something as simple as the disorder in the garage, overstuffed closets, piles of papers and bills on the desk, an overgrown yard, or some other kind of clutter that needs to be attended to.

Now reflect on the following questions:

- Do any of your judgments about these things come from the past?
- Are you creating a negative view of yourself because of these things?
- Do the judgments imply you are a bad or less worthy person?
- How do the judgments make you feel?
- Do the judgments affect your ability to act effectively or to clearly see the situation and the necessary next steps?
- Does discerning, as opposed to judging, allow you to look at the situation with more perspective and not get bogged down in self-judgment and conclusions about what all these things mean about you as a person?
- Does discernment allow you to view these things more neutrally — as simply tasks to be done,

issues to be looked at, situations to be managed, or jobs you may need assistance with?

Can you see the difference between approaching a situation with judgment and viewing it with discernment? In life we often flit back and forth between both perspectives. Our task is to note the judgments and then summon our ability to discern what the situation is and what response it requires. Try to apply this principle to any challenge in life. First notice the situation, then note the reaction, judgments, or shaming from the critic. Then stop listening to the critic and set about using your discernment to determine what is needed. By doing this, you are freeing up the potential of your discriminating mind.

PART TWO

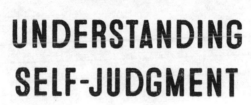

UNDERSTANDING SELF-JUDGMENT

IT'S ABOUT *YOU*, STUPID!

◄▬ ▬►

How the Critic Attacks Your Innate Value

A good review from the critics is just another stay of execution.

— DUSTIN HOFFMAN

The key issue with the inner critic, and the reason it is so important to address it, is that the critic fundamentally attacks your sense of self worth. This may not be the most obvious thing the critic does, so let me illustrate with a story that a student reported to me:

One Friday night Alex is getting ready for his good friend Josh's fortieth birthday party. Even though he cares deeply about his friend, Alex has left it to the last minute to get him a present. So he's rushing around, stuck in rush-hour traffic in downtown Manhattan, chastising himself for not getting a present sooner. He justifies the last-minute stress by telling himself it's worth it for this particular friend. And besides, he would feel terrible showing up at the party empty-handed.

The only thing Josh said he wanted was a particular golf club. Unfortunately, the golf store is sold out of them, and it will take a week for new stock to arrive. Alex again berates himself for not having taken care of it earlier, since Josh specified exactly what he wanted and Alex knows he wants for little else. There are not many second-best options.

So Alex puts a golf club on order, tries to conjure up his best excuse, and heads home to get ready and check the invitation for the details of where the party is being held. To his astonishment, he sees that Josh's birthday fell on a Thursday and the celebration was the night before.

You can imagine the scene in Alex's head. Not only did he screw up with the present, but he missed the all-important celebration. All because he didn't take the time to read the invitation carefully or put it in his calendar. He already feels bad about missing the chance to celebrate his friend's birthday. But then, right on cue, the critic starts to rev up its engines. This is a perfect storm for the judge to step onto the scene.

No sooner does Alex realize his error than the judgments start coming, thick and fast. First the critic is on his case for being unorganized. "How could you not simply read the invitation and write down the date correctly?" it demands. The critic then brings in as evidence all the other things Alex has screwed up. All the other forgotten birthdays, the missed wedding anniversaries, the times he has been late for a meeting or missed a flight. Suddenly, Alex starts feeling like a hopeless case, a half-wit who couldn't even tie his own shoelaces. The critic expands the particular into the universal and makes him feel terrible.

What is important to note is that the attack isn't simply a critique of his efficiency, but an assertion that he is a bad and worthless person. And the judge doesn't stop there. It then begins an assault on his value as a friend. "How could you miss one of your best friend's most important days?" Then the judge begins to broaden the attack: Does he really value friendship as much as he says he does? Is he really there for his buddies if he can miss such a key event? Isn't he just lost in his own world, his own selfish interests? Doesn't a real friend show up, come hell or high water? Isn't friendship built on shared memories and experiences?

You can imagine how Alex is now feeling. The double whammy of being attacked as both disorganized and an unworthy friend starts to sink Alex down into the mire. The critic may also bring in the perspective of history and say something like: "You have always been bad at attending to details and cannot be trusted. Look at how many things you've spaced out on in the past. You're basically unreliable. And given how long this has been going on, it's never going to change. You will probably always be undependable. You're basically a hopeless case. Its surprising you have any friends left. Look at all those other times you let people down."

So what started as a simple calendar error, something any one of us can do, given our complex lives and fractured attention, has grown into an outright assault on the heart and soul of Alex. It is fine to point out the occasional errors we make, and offer some constructive criticism on how we can attend to details better in the future. It is a different order of magnitude when the critic attacks our basic goodness.

Educational psychologists have known for a long time how important it is, when giving criticism, to separate the person from the action. This is the important difference between person- and process-centered criticism or praise. When we tell a child they are bad because they skipped school or didn't turn in their homework, we are forgetting the important rule of separating the action from the person. The child internalizes the idea that they are a bad person, rather than understanding that the action is what is under scrutiny.

Instead of telling our children that they are good boys and girls all the time, we need to remember to separate their actions from who they are. We can praise their good study habits, great athletic performance, or the fact that they remember to say "please" and "thank you." But that is very different from telling them they are a good boy or girl for doing so. The inference from such feedback is that when they don't do those things, they are no longer good. This may sound simplistic, but it is the way we develop our self-image and identity.

Unfortunately for us, the critic makes the same mistake parents often do. Rather than telling Alex how unfortunate it is that he overlooked the details on an invitation and how he needs to pay closer attention to details, the judge instead implies that for doing so, Alex is a bad person, perhaps even unworthy of friendship. You can see how different those two perspectives are.

So what is key for Alex is separating the critique of his actions from his worth as a human being. He needs to understand there is something that may need improvement in terms of his attention to detail and at the same time fend off the judge's assessment of him as a person. If he can do that, he can learn from his mistakes. If he can't, he will continue to feel bad, unworthy, and ashamed, and he will be no less likely to repeat the same mistakes.

If we can learn to uncouple the action, however bad, from the person, then we can find the space to navigate the terrain of judgment without our self-esteem collapsing. We can instead see clearly what happened, what was or wasn't okay, and take suitable action to change our behavior rather than sinking into hopelessness and self-hatred. That approach is the doorway to transformation.

⟵ PRACTICE ⟶

Connecting with Your Inherent Value

For this practice you will do a reflective meditation.

1. Find a place where you can be undisturbed for at least ten minutes. Sitting in a chair where you can be upright yet relaxed, assume a comfortable posture. Allow your body to be at ease.

2. Gently close your eyes and turn your attention first to your breath. Then shift your awareness to the various sensations throughout your body.

3. Once you feel settled and present, slowly begin to reflect on the physical functions your body performs. Acknowledge your heart beating, your lungs breathing, your intestines digesting, your brain thinking. Can you feel a sense of appreciation for your body and all it does? Your body, like every other physical being on earth, deserves to be; it has a rightful place on this planet. It is worthy, without having to do anything except simply be here.

4. Now reflect on the fact that you are unique on this earth. Can you see how you — your body, heart, and mind — are completely original, one of a kind, unrepeatable? You have value and worth simply by existing, just as everything else in this world does. What you do and say, the job you do,

whether you are a parent or not, how wealthy or smart you are — these are all secondary to your inherent, innate worth. A single daffodil adds value, even in a field of a million daffodils; it has value just by existing. It is beautiful in and of itself. Can you feel the same way about yourself?

5. Take a few moments to reflect on all the ways you express innate goodness quite naturally. These can be things as simple as holding a door open for someone; letting another car in front of you in traffic; feeding the birds in winter; calling a friend or family member who you know is having a hard time; complimenting others; or all the ways you may be spontaneously kind to strangers and generous to the people you know. Sense how all these kinds of actions are expressions of the goodness and inherent value of your nature.

6. When you feel ready to end this meditation, slowly open your eyes, and gently move and stretch.

This is probably a different way to look at yourself than you are used to. So you may encounter resistance, or even scorn, from the judging mind. If that happens, notice the thoughts but review the preceding paragraphs in this meditation, reading one at a time and letting yourself reflect on the words. You may need to do this practice several times to connect with the essence of what it is pointing to.

See if you can bring to mind this reflection on your inherent value at different times of your day. Try to recall it particularly when your critic is railing at you.

You can try using a simple phrase as a mantra that you

repeat to yourself — for example: "I am enough," "I am fine just as I am," or "I have value just by being alive." Or you can offer yourself an aspirational phrase like "May I know my own worth" or "May I always stay connected to my inherent value." At first these phrases may ring hollow. However, if you repeat them slowly and genuinely over time, they can begin to take root, just as a plant can grow even in rocky soil.

CHAPTER TEN

THE MANTRA OF "NOT ENOUGH"

◄ ► ▬

Knowing When Enough Is Enough

Perfectionism is a self-destructive and addictive belief system that fuels this primary thought: "If I look perfect, live perfectly, and do everything perfectly, I can avoid or minimize the painful feelings of shame, judgment, and blame."

— BRENÉ BROWN

In my work as a mindfulness consultant, I go into companies and train people to develop awareness and presence. They then apply those mindfulness skills to improve the way they work, manage, make decisions, give presentations, and communicate with others. Lands Capital was one such company. Based in New York, it was a successful tech hedge fund that was growing after the dot-com crash.

One day I walked in to do some mindfulness coaching for several members of the executive team, and there was a particularly jubilant air in the office. I heard that one of the traders, James, had completed a very successful trade he had been working on for months that netted almost thirty million dollars for the company that day. Not too bad! I had a meeting scheduled with

James in the afternoon and was looking forward to congratulating him on his success. I imagined he would be feeling quite satisfied with himself.

Much to my surprise, when I walked into his office, I saw him looking stressed and troubled. Where was the joy of a successful trader who had made the company and himself a windfall? As we talked, I began to unpack the story. He told me about his research on this particular investment. He had been tracking this company for a while, but rather than feel fantastic about his trading, he felt angst.

He explained that if he had just bought when he first had the hunch to do so, and if he'd only hung on for a few hours more that day, he would have made several million dollars more. So unfortunately for James, he was unable to relax into the good work he had done, because, according to his estimate, he could have done much better.

Such is the way of the critic. It's never enough. No matter what we do, it always reminds us we could do more, be better, achieve something greater. It robs us of the satisfaction of our accomplishments. How many great, talented musicians, artists, entrepreneurs, parents, teachers, and countless others have been haunted by the sense of "not enough"? How far are we from grasping the words of Taoist philosopher Lao-tzu, who wrote, "Those who know when enough is enough, have enough, and will never want for more"?

This mantra of "not enough" is pervasive. It's what drives much of industrialized society and the free market. It's part of the hedonistic treadmill at the heart of materialist culture. Driven by a belief in scarcity, we strive for more. We try to get more of anything. You name it — bigger houses, higher salaries, faster cars, newer gadgets, bigger 401(k)'s, and more and more stuff to fill our houses, basements, and storage units! A Ford truck ad sums it up: riffing on New Age values and materialism, the slogan goes, "To be one with everything, you gotta have one of everything!"

And the mantra of "not enough" gets applied not just to our stuff, but to our bodies too. This fuels a host of painful feelings — about not being slim enough, fit enough, strong enough, healthy enough, pretty enough, young enough. These feelings can result in an endless project of physical self-improvement and a painful rejection of how our body actually is.

If we listen to that voice preaching scarcity, a bitter, panicked search for more ensues. The search is stressful and endless, and leads to eating disorders, workaholism, credit card debt, self-harm, and addiction. It fosters an obsession with making money at all costs and with building muscle or losing weight without regard for the impact on our health. It drives people to consume, hoard, and spend themselves into poverty. And it leads to terrible tragedy when there is a sudden loss of the things we compulsively seek, as happens during a financial collapse. The ability to cope with such loss is too much for some. Suicide rates went up exponentially after the financial collapses of 1929 and 2008.

Perhaps more important is what happens when we turn this sense of scarcity to our inner world, to who we are in our essence. One of the most pervasive inner voices is the one that tells people that whatever they do, whatever they are, is not enough. Professors at Harvard don't feel smart enough; successful traders don't feel sharp enough; palliative-care nurses don't feel caring enough; writers don't feel eloquent enough. An important question to ask yourself is, "What is my particular 'not enough' mantra?"

In this paradigm there is no firm ground on which to rest. No time to enjoy a natural contentment with what we have or with what is here. It leads to an inner restlessness, a constant existential itch, a hunger that can't be quenched. In Indian cosmology this is known as the "hungry ghost" state. Hungry ghosts have big bellies and small mouths, and whatever they eat burns. So they are left with constant hunger. This state makes it hard to be with ourselves since we are constantly distracted by an inner lack.

Think about what happens when you are swept up in that state of not-enoughness. It feels empty, hollow, and unpleasant. It's not easy to deal with this sense of deficiency, which we sometimes experience as a hole in our chest or belly. The associations that come with the experience make it doubly difficult. When we were children, to our young brains this feeling of lack could be associated with not being likable or wanted. If we are not enough, we reasoned, then people may not like us or, worse still, we may lose love. And to a young person the possible withdrawal of affection and approval is terrifying.

In response to these feelings of lack, we do everything we can to fill the perceived void, to make sure any withdrawal of love doesn't happen, or at least doesn't last. We begin that desperate attempt to achieve whatever we think will guarantee affection, attention, and praise, be it good grades, good athletic performance, or simply being "good." And the critic makes sure we don't stop, as it attempts to figure out the best way to maximize that flow of approval and love.

A cousin of the "not enough" mantra is the habit of comparing. The critic often employs this equally damaging weapon, reminding you there is always someone smarter, younger, sharper, kinder, or more successful than you. And because of that, you are again not good enough and should try harder. If you buy into the perspective of the comparing mind, you set yourself up for a life of misery. The mind-set of comparison entrenches the view that there is always more to do, always ways to improve, and that the road is an endless uphill trudge. There is never peace of mind with the comparing mind, period. Even if you are on the winning end of the comparing scale, your win is always tenuous, vulnerable to the next person to come along who is smarter, younger, or cuter.

That's not to deny the value of working on ourselves. The key is to approach that task not from a perspective of deficiency, but from the perspective of knowing that we have vast potential already within us that is there for the taking if we so choose. As Zen teacher Suzuki Roshi once said, "Each of you is perfect the way you are...*and* you can use a little improvement." That is a far more benevolent and inspiring model than feeling that we have to pull ourselves up by our bootstraps because we are just not up to snuff. In this more balanced paradigm, the self-improvement can be fun — a journey full of adventure, with many secrets to discover and various skills to grow into.

A key strategy for counteracting the malaise of not-enoughness is to cultivate the practice of gratitude. For when we are feeling grateful, we can't also be feeling deficient. Gratitude by its very nature has a sense of fullness and wholeness within it.

Gratitude is one of my favorite practices and reflections. When I shift from a feeling of lack to remembering all the things, people, gifts, and opportunities I have in my life, it transforms my sense of deficiency into one of fullness and appreciation for life and its blessings. This is possible for anyone at any time.

We can also turn that attitude of gratefulness toward ourselves to counter any feelings of scarcity within. How would you feel if you took a few moments to thank your feet for all the hard work they do in supporting you and getting you around? How about a moment to appreciate your heart, which beats millions of times in the course of your life? And what about your amazing senses — your eyes, which allow you to take in the marvelous sights of the world, or your ears, which open you up to a world of sound?

I particularly enjoy extending my gratitude to places and

people I might not ordinarily think about. For example, when I'm driving, I take a few moments to appreciate the smoothness of the road and all the people who worked hard to create that. Or when I flush my toilet, I appreciate all the workers who take care of the sewage systems. Or when I hear sirens, I appreciate the emergency crews who dedicate their lives to helping others. Sometimes it is just simple things, like feeling grateful for the potters who made the cup I drink my tea out of every morning.

I find that when I practice gratitude, it warms my heart and makes the world seem more full, textured, multicolored. It allows me to count my blessings and feel a sense of fullness rather than lack.

➤ PRACTICE ➤
Cultivating Gratitude

You can do this exercise either as a written reflection, a meditation, or both. Begin by turning your attention to all the things you are grateful for, including:

- All that you have right now
- What is already right here
- All the things you are freely given

Let your stream of consciousness flow as you allow your mind to open and wander to all the things, people, places, and experiences you are grateful for.

You may discover that the more you do this exercise, the more gratitude begins to flow. Sometimes you may feel a waterfall of gratitude for things you have never considered. You might start with appreciating your garden, then feel appreciation for the paving stones there and the people who laid them, the bugs in the soil keeping the plants healthy, or all the people who have cultivated and harvested seeds for thousands of years. This may take you to feeling thankful for all the people who made your clothes from as far away as China or Brazil, to the zipper makers and people who sewed buttons on your shirt, and those who dyed those same clothes.

This might take you to the other aspects of gratitude — appreciating what is right here and seeing how things are given to you. You may, for instance, recollect how the elements are always here — the air, water, earth, and heat of the sun. Perhaps you may feel appreciation for gravity, which allows us and everything to stay rooted right here and the rain to shower the land all around us. Or you may appreciate the changing seasons and the beauty and variation that come with them.

Or you may begin to feel how much you are given every moment: the warm sun on your face, the hard work of the pollinating bees and insects that allow flowers and crops to grow, or the way clouds release their load of rain, nourishing the land and forests and cleansing the streets. Or the way wildflowers and grasses simply spring up in the most unlikely places in the city to provide beauty and delight.

Keep doing this as a daily practice, turning your mind to all that is here, full, complete, and offering itself freely, and notice how this starts to erode the mind-set of scarcity. Enjoy!

CHAPTER ELEVEN

20/20 HINDSIGHT

◄ ►

How the Critic Fuels Regret

We judge ourselves by what we feel capable of doing, while others judge us by what we have already done.

— HENRY WADSWORTH LONGFELLOW

ow many times have you made a plan, or gotten swept up in an impulse buy or extravagant purchase, then lived to regret the decision? There's a reason for the expression "buyer's remorse." What about all the things you've said to loved ones in the heat of the moment that you wish you could take back? Did you have relationships in your teens or twenties and later wonder how you could have ever gone out with that person? Do you sometimes look at your calendar and regret booking yourself so solid and saying yes to all those projects?

Who hasn't made a decision and later wished they had done something different? It seems to be part of life. It is bad enough to feel you made a wrong decision. As bad as that is, it's even worse when your critic doesn't let you forget you "messed up" because you moved to a company that went belly up, bet on a losing stock, or chose a crazy person to date. How long has your critic been berating you for decisions you made years ago? How much unnecessary pain has that caused?

Regret is one of the stickiest places in my own psyche. My critic has been quite vocal about all the supposedly incorrect decisions I've made in the past, which makes it harder to make a clear decision without fearing the critic's wrath. "What if I make the 'wrong' choice?" I hear my mind say in anticipation of an upcoming dilemma.

Like many who have devoted their lives to inner spiritual work and not so much to making money, I have been burned a few times in my somewhat amateur investing attempts. Once in the dot-com crash in 2000, and again in the real estate crash in 2008. Predictably, my critic has something to say about my relationship to money — that I'm not to be trusted in that department. (Since that time I have mostly let others with more experience and skill in financial matters do the investing for me!)

You could say the critic has a valid point, given my less-than-lucrative attempts at investing. The problem, however, is what's implied in its critique: shame, guilt, and the assessment that I'm a failure with money and, by extension, everything else. The challenging thing about the critic's attacks is the emotional legacy they leave behind, such as fear and paralysis when it comes to making choices, and a sense of inadequacy.

Since the critic always has the unfair advantage of 20/20 vision, it is easy for it to dole out judgments about past choices regarding money, career, or relationships. It is not hard, in hindsight, to say what you should or shouldn't have done, what would have been a smarter choice regarding a relationship, a new job, an investment, or a secondhand car.

Hindsight gives us the perspective we just don't have when making a decision. And it is pointless, if not downright unfair, to blame ourselves in hindsight. Learning from past errors is, of course, necessary. But the blame-and-shame game is unnecessary and unhelpful.

Sometimes the critic thinks that if it berates us enough, we won't make the same mistake again. In my experience this is rarely true. No matter how much the critic judges me for moves I've made in the past, it doesn't help with the next decision. In fact, the critic's judgments make it more difficult to make good decisions in the future because they cloud our thinking with fear and hopelessness about the decision-making process.

There is no necessarily right or wrong decision. What seems like a good thing at one moment may be a bad thing from another perspective and vice versa. Using DDT to eradicate malaria in the United States seemed like a good idea at the time. But now we know the impact of its toxic fallout. It almost obliterated many species of birds, including the bald eagle. From the vantage point of today, we can see it was a shortsighted idea.

It is also important to remember that we try to do the best we can with the information and resources at hand. That's true of every decision we've ever made, no matter how bad it turned out to be. If we could have done better, we would have done so. It doesn't help to thrash ourselves for not knowing better; we have to give ourselves the benefit of the doubt. To understand this is very liberating; it frees us from the torment of recrimination.

The ability to let go also helps mitigate the force of the critic, which, like other aspects of the ego, wants and needs control. It believes that if it can control things, it can manage situations so we get what we need and avoid what is threatening. However, there are far too many factors outside our control to know for sure which way the stock or housing market will go or how a relationship may unfold. Yes, we could do better and make better choices if we had a crystal ball, but we don't have that luxury.

Instead life demands that we put our stake in the ground, make our choice, and do our best to meet whatever actually happens. Of course, we would like a particular outcome, but we don't need to chastise ourselves when things don't go our way. Ideally, we practice letting go of trying to control experience, situations, and people because we realize that is never really possible anyway. We trust that we made the best decision we could at the time, we see what happens, and we learn. And if necessary, we let go.

It's important to stress that regrets resulting from 20/20 hindsight are not easy to be with. They are unpleasant, and made worse by our aversion to both the feeling and the memory that triggers it. The experience is felt as a heaviness in the body. In the mind we may feel it as fogginess and a torrent of self-judging thoughts. Emotionally we may notice it as a contraction in our heart.

The challenge with a difficult experience like regret is to have the courage to take our attention close to it and feel it, without the additional layer of self-reproach. When we can get to the root of regret, and separate the critic from the experience, we fully learn from our actions. Then we can have genuine remorse, where we see the error of our ways and form an intention not to go down the same road again. This brings a freedom that is not dragged down by the burden of chastising ourselves.

⟶ PRACTICE ⟵
Letting Go of Regrets

If you are plagued by regret and your inner critic is always on your case about past decisions, then this would be a useful practice.

In your journal or on a piece of paper, write down one

or more things you regret. Then select one of these items (if there's more than one, choose one of the least heavy). Call to mind the experience related to that particular regret — the situation, the time, the characters, and any other memory of the experience. Reflect on why you chose the particular course of action you did.

Then reflect on the following bits of wisdom:

- We can't undo the past.
- Everything always looks clearer with 20/20 hindsight.
- You are not clairvoyant and could not have predicted what the future would bring.
- You always did the best you could, given the experience, knowledge, and information you had at the time.
- Life couldn't have happened any other way.
- What was, was, and it cannot be changed.
- Trying to remake the past is pointless and painful.
- Peace comes from reconciling yourself to what is and what was.
- Peace comes from letting go of regrets about past actions.

As you ponder these principles, see if you can apply them to your situation. Can you see how it could not have been any other way? Can you see that you were always doing the best you could, given your knowledge and abilities at the time? When you have reflected sufficiently, see if it's possible to put the sword of blame down. Can you offer yourself some forgiveness for all that you did and said?

Work with these principles each time the critic gets on your case about a past decision. And in the future, practice making the best decision you can, then let go of any urge to rehash the decision in your mind. Simply rest in the decision you made, without any self-recrimination. See if you can apply this approach to the decisions in your life so you can free yourself from the torment of regret and indecision.

CHAPTER TWELVE

THE INNER BOARDROOM

— ◄ ► —

Understanding the Voices in Your Head

Court not the critic's smile nor dread his frown.

— SIR WALTER SCOTT

In a training course I was leading, a participant named Andrew, a high school teacher from Ohio, bemoaned the noisy boss that lived inside his head. It was always giving him a hard time and telling him he was doing things wrong, particularly when it came to his teaching. I sympathized with him and liked his metaphor for the inner critic. It is like someone has camped out in the living room and sits around all day giving you orders and critiquing everything you do.

Later in the course someone said that Andrew was lucky in that he only had one boss in his head. Samantha, new in her role as CEO at an investment firm in Dallas, felt like the whole boardroom was inside her head, each board member with their different judgments and critiques of what she did and said.

When we look at the voice of the critic, we see there are multiple streams of critical thoughts, or "personalities," in our mind.
Some refer to it as the "inner boardroom" — a committee that is
always having a meeting about us and issuing commands — or
liken it to a cast of characters in a play who are busy making judgments about everything we do.

As with any boardroom, it is important to get to know all the
voices, hear what each one is saying, and learn how to work with
them skillfully. So if you were to take a look, what would *you* find
inside that eleven-pound mass of flesh we call the brain or inside
that mysterious thing we call the mind? How many voices, subpersonalities, and critical characters do you haul around? As the
saying goes, "Wherever you go, there you are!" But a more accurate phrase would be "Wherever you go, there the judges are!"
Do you notice how they follow you around? Even when you go
on vacation, you don't escape: the committee is judging you on
how you look on the beach, what you eat, or how much you drink.

What are some of the typical members of the boardroom?
First there is usually a board chair, the more dominant one who
shouts the loudest, controls the proceedings, and has the last
word. It can be an aggressive voice. It likes to give orders, especially about the big-picture direction of your life and how you are
managing resources.

Then there is the coach, which is a little more encouraging
and positive — the voice that says, "You can do it. Just try harder,
work smarter, tend to this, adjust that." It's often reminding you
to keep tinkering because you are not doing it quite right. The
coach insists you need it to tell you what to do, because you'd be
lost on your own.

The treasurer is the one critiquing you for not dealing with
money effectively enough. It's telling you that you need to plan

better, make better financial decisions, save more, work harder, stop spending so liberally, and be more cautious, or take more calculated risks, when making investments.

An interesting board member is what I call the dilettante. It's the pleasure seeker in the crowd. This isn't someone you normally associate with the downer vibe of the critic. It's the one who is on your case if you are not having enough fun, getting enough pleasure, or doing enough playful things. It's reprimanding you if you deprive yourself of pleasure as a reward for all your hard work.

Not half as fun is the perfectionist. This persona is never happy. No matter how hard you try, it's just not good enough, precise enough, smart enough. It is so easy to fail the test of its impossibly high standards. In fact, you are doomed to fail, as it is impossible to reach perfection and satisfy this board member. It's the voice that has the mantra of "not good enough" woven into it. It is a guaranteed source of unhappiness.

Another common voice is the taskmaster, or what some call the tyrant. This one is a toughie. This voice doesn't allow you to let up, take a break, or relax. It's the voice that comes when you are having a siesta, sleeping in, watching your favorite HBO series, or enjoying a drink. It reminds you of all the tasks left to do, all the emails not replied to, and the things piling up on your to-do list that you said you would get to but haven't. This voice pesters you when you appear to slack off. It never lets you rest. It's a slave driver. It's exhausting when you're under its thumb.

Do you recognize this cast of characters? What others do you have percolating inside? Perhaps the doomsday voice reminding you that it's all going to fail. Or what about the killjoy, which always comes along and tells you something that just saps your spirit. Then there is the saboteur, the one that gets you to engage in self-sabotage, undermines all your best efforts, keeps ensuring you arrive late, don't respond in time, and say the inappropriate thing. And then happily chastises you for doing so.

It is a cast of actors Disney could make a movie with, but it's not a film I'd want to see. Yet, sadly, we listen to these inner reality-radio shows every day of our lives, with only occasional changes in the sad cast. How long will we keep listening to this repetitive junk, giving it attention and feeling miserable?

As François Fénelon, a Christian cleric and writer, once noted, "We only perceive the malady when the cure begins." When we bring the voices of our inner boardroom into the light of day, under the scrutiny of awareness, we can begin to be "cured," or at least begin the process of healing. So although it can be demoralizing to realize how many negative voices lie within, it is essential to shine the light of awareness on them.

Once the boardroom is in view, we can begin inquiring into all these voices. What are the names and roles of these characters? Which one do you give the most attention to? Which one are you most afraid of or influenced by? What happens when they are quiet? How do you feel when they leave you alone and you're free of their demands? And perhaps the key question: Do you believe what they are telling you, and follow their advice?

Most importantly, notice how you can observe all these voices from the perspective of mindfulness. Awareness lets you bring attention to these voices without getting caught up in what they have to say. It allows you to see them from a third-person perspective, as if you were watching someone else's movie, and therefore be less affected by them. (You will learn more about the power and role of mindfulness in chapter 16.) You can view these characters as talking heads on a TV with the volume muted, knowing they are there, but not listening to or caring about what they have to say.

PRACTICE

Identifying Your Inner Boardroom

It is important to begin to identify the board members that regularly show up, and to examine the voices of the various characters that bark orders, judgments, and criticisms at you.

Start by writing out an exhaustive list of all these challenging characters, giving each one a name: Do you have the killjoy, persecutor, controller, underminer, fault finder, abuser? Or perhaps a coach, judge, perfectionist, taskmaster, tyrant, penny-pincher, nitpicker, or simply a critic? Notice what happens when you name them.

Try to bring them to life to make them more real. If they were people, what would they look like? How would they dress and act? The more you can identify, name, and give a playful characterization to these characters, the easier it will be to recognize them when they start playing their tune, and it will also help you hold them with more lightness.

Now identify the specific judgments that come from each member of your inner boardroom. What is each voice saying, asking, demanding, critiquing? Perhaps one (or more) of them is mean, insulting, and berating about your health, weight, looks, intelligence, work, or relationships. Once you have identified the judgments, take some time to reflect on them: Are these judgments fair, helpful, or even true? Notice what happens when you examine the judgments with more objectivity.

Next reflect on what may lie behind each judgment. Each voice may have a particular concern or fear and, in its own rather crude way, may be trying to protect you from harm or help you with something. What concern or fear could be at the root of the board member's judgment? For instance, the treasurer may be afraid you will be irresponsible with money. It is perhaps driven by concerns about financial security and a desire for you to take care of business so you can be on a more sound financial footing. The eating coach may be trying to protect you against the shame you would feel about being overweight, so it issues orders about what not to eat, in an attempt to keep you from gaining weight.

Although they may be trying to protect you, such harsh, controlling voices — and their judgments — not only are unhelpful, but can actually be counterproductive. They often leave you feeling ashamed and guilty. And as a result, you may do the very thing they are trying to protect you against, such as overeating.

Once you have explored the boardroom's underlying and perhaps positive motivations, reflect on what would be more useful than harsh judgments and condemnations as a way of encouraging you to take positive action or wholesome next steps. For each judgment you identified, write out a more constructive way to express the board member's concern and the positive action or step you could take to address it.

CHAPTER THIRTEEN

THE CRITIC'S REVOLVING DOOR

◄ ►

What Goes Out Must Go In

If we had no faults, we should not take so much pleasure in noting those of others.

— FRANÇOIS DE LA ROCHEFOUCAULD

Some years ago I was teaching a course in a hospital in Shef-field, England. There was a psychiatrist in the course who was in his fifties and who, although cordial on the surface, could be quite vicious in his attacks on others in the group. Out of the blue, he would issue scathing judgments about their errors. What was challenging for his colleagues was that they could never be sure when to expect one of his barbed attacks.

Later I came to work with him, in a coaching format. I discovered his life was tormented by his own vicious attacks on himself. Growing up in a critical family, he felt that he never lived up to their expectations. His father — ironically, a judge in a local court — had hoped his son would follow him into law. To his disappointment, his son did not, and he did not hide his disdain for his son's career choice.

As a consequence, the psychiatrist had internalized this culture of judgment and was unforgiving of even the slightest error in himself or others. He lived his life under the oppressive reach of the critic's hand. It had turned his life into a narrow hell where nothing he did was right, no matter how successful he was in medicine. What he didn't see was how he turned that same critique toward everyone around him, literally scaring them away. It was no wonder he felt sad and lonely.

Have you ever wondered what it's like at home for the most judgmental person you know at the office? Rest assured it wouldn't be all quiet. For the most part, what goes out goes in; if someone is outwardly critical, they are most likely also turning the screw on themselves when there is no one else around to take aim at.

However, people do tend to lean more in one direction than the other — either outward or inward — when judging. Take a look at your own mind and see if that is so. Do you tend to judge yourself or others more, or is it about even? Or do the judgments just go whichever way the critic is looking?

It is important to understand your mental habits because the more you practice a habit, the more entrenched it becomes. If your habit is to judge (whether internally or externally), guess what becomes the norm? The key point here is that we do not want to strengthen the critic's fundamentally problematic point of view. Unlike a person exercising discernment, the critic attacks whoever falls under its scrutiny. That is a terrible fate to befall anyone. It is most dire when done to oneself, which is where the guillotine will inevitably fall if we keep up the habit of judging others.

So how do you interrupt this habit? The primary line of defense is simply to notice that it's there. When seeing this habit with mindful awareness, we can note it for what it is — merely thoughts, and points of view, that are not necessarily true. We can let go of the thoughts and shift our attention to something else.

An effective counterpoint to habitual negative fixation is to focus on the positive. To look for what is right or wholesome in others or oneself and to focus on those good qualities. That doesn't mean we throw out discernment; it just means we don't give preference to the negative. It is remarkable how that small shift can begin to bring more light into your inner and outer world.

What would it be like for you to look at the world, and the people in it, with more of a focus on the light, on what is positive and right? How would that change your state of mind? Perhaps it would lead you to see yourself in the same way — not as someone with a list of faults as long as your arm, but as someone who has strengths, talents, gifts, and a good heart.

⟩⟩ PRACTICE ⟩⟩

Finding the Positive in Others

This is a practice you can do as you go about your day and encounter people. I try to do this whenever someone enters my presence, whether in the office, the bus, a café, or a store. It shifts my perspective from one of fear, caution, or anxiety to one of greater warmth, interest, and positivity.

Next time you are in a public place and you look at someone, notice first what your normal, habitual pattern is. Do you see their faults, what is wrong with them, and all the ways you might critique their dress, weight, hair, conversation, and so on?

Then, to shift the negatively oriented judging habit, try to see one positive quality about the person. What attribute of theirs — a skill, quality, action, or something in their speech, dress, or manner — can you appreciate? Observe what happens when you turn your attention to that aspect of them. How does it make you feel? Does it feel genuine or forced? Is there any judgment that this is naive or doesn't take in the whole picture? Or does it allow you to move from a critical orientation to one that is more life affirming or positive?

Try to do this for a specific period of time, such as ten minutes, or for an entire bus ride, or throughout a meeting at work. You can also try doing this while at a family dinner, or when shopping, standing in line, or at a sports event. Notice how it can change your mood and the way you feel about the people around you.

Try bringing the same perspective to yourself as you go through the day. What would it be like to turn your attention to your positive qualities, actions, and strengths? Notice how this too shifts the bias from what is wrong to what is actually okay and positive.

CHAPTER FOURTEEN

THE IMPACT OF THE CRITIC

━◄ ►━

How Judgments Affect Us

Instead of spending our lives running towards our dreams, we are often running away from a fear of failure or a fear of criticism.

— ERIC WRIGHT

Steve was an up-and-coming high school basketball player who had just made it to the play-offs in his school's regional championship in the San Francisco Bay Area. He was only seventeen yet had inherited a very critical judge from his high-achieving parents, who were both psychologists. He was hoping to get a scholarship for a University of California college the following year.

In a crucial game, he was given the ball with seven seconds left to make the winning shot. Nerves got to him, and he missed. He was mortified because his team didn't make it through the play-offs. During a coaching session, he recalled how he felt an unprecedented heaviness and exhaustion as he walked home. It was like he was moving through molasses. His head felt foggy, and he could barely think straight. An air of hopelessness engulfed him. He was feeling the assault of his critic affecting him on many levels. It took some time to shake off the physical impact of his judge crucifying him for missing that critical shot.

Have you ever left an event where you had to perform — a sports event, work presentation, school exam, or important conversation — but didn't perform well, then wondered later that day why you were feeling so physically exhausted? Why you felt unusually tired and foggy brained, or emotionally low?

These are common symptoms of the critic, and they can wreak havoc in your life if they go unnoticed. The critic can affect you on many levels. There is the mental level, where it uses words to shame and judge, and where you may feel confused by or preoccupied with the critic's words. But it can also impact you on a physical, emotional, or energetic level. Once you start to recognize the physiological symptoms, you can trace them backward to find the judgment at their root and release it.

One of the more common effects of the critic is a brain fog that leaves you feeling mentally dull and murky. It is as if your brain is stuck in the wrong gear and the judgments are quietly whirring just below your perceptual threshold, gnawing away at you and draining precious mental resources. In this state of mind it can be difficult to think clearly or make decisions. It can feel like your brain is frozen and you've lost the antifreeze.

When I notice this kind of brain fog, I attempt to see what kind of judgment might be festering in the murky waters of my mind. I will try to verbalize it to myself, even if I'm just guessing. And once the judgment is brought into the cold light of day, I can begin to work with it cognitively and begin to free myself from its grip, rather than letting it clog up my mind.

One place the critic tends to be particularly corrosive, and where its impact is felt on both the physical and energetic levels, is in raising children. I have seen female clients who after successful careers let go of climbing the career ladder in order to raise a family. It is often a hard adjustment going from success and status in business to managing the chaos of raising kids. As any parent will attest, with parenting it is not uncommon to feel a sense of never doing it right, not being good enough, or not quite knowing what to do with the tantrums, sibling rivalries, teenage angst, and other challenges of raising children.

Jean, a homemaker with a well-developed inner critic, grew up in a household where her mother took great pride in the cleanliness and order of her house, despite having to raise five children on a limited income. Jean told me what can happen when her husband comes home from work. Often she is exhausted at the end of the day from raising and homeschooling her three kids, who are under nine years of age. When her husband arrives, the house is usually a mess, strewn with toys, books, and residue of the day's activity with the kids. If he makes an innocent comment about not being able to find something in the chaos, she easily internalizes that as judgment.

Jean can then quickly spin into feeling that her whole day didn't matter. All the good she did in schooling her three kids seems irrelevant — she feels unworthy as a homemaker due to the mess and chaos at home. Irrational, but not uncommon. She remembers how her mother would never have let such a mess be seen by anyone, let alone her husband. Such a process, she says, can easily trigger an emotional plunge, culminating in a universal sense of feeling "bad." Everything then becomes filtered through this veil of unworthiness.

Being without the usual support the ego gets from being successful at work, stay-at-home mothers and fathers commonly carry a sense of not being good enough parents. They can experience the impact of this judgment emotionally as a heaviness, a

dullness, a sinking feeling. It can also cause a sense of hopelessness that feels like a heavy, lingering mist. This burden dulls the
experience of anything else, so much so that it can feel like a mild
depression.

I encourage my clients to try to express their emotions in
words — to articulate the voice, critique, judgment, or negative
message they may be unconsciously telling themselves and that
may lie behind their heavy feelings. Once the feeling or state is
verbalized, they have something clearer to work on, inquire into,
challenge, or understand.

Sometimes an unnoticed self-judgment triggers more of an
energetic contraction or collapse. We can feel this physically as
a heaviness or lack of energy. This can easily happen when we
have just left an important conversation or a meeting with our
boss where we said the "wrong" thing. Afterward we may suddenly feel a sense of lethargy, as if we were ready for sleep, that
comes from a critic attack we didn't notice. If we ask ourselves
what the judgment was that we didn't catch, we might realize the
critic was saying, "It's all hopeless. You messed up. Your boss is
going to think you're a fool." From this point of view everything
looks like an uphill battle.

The remedy for this pattern is, again, to articulate what the
thought or judgment is that is expressing itself as physical fatigue
and heaviness. Once we put it into words, we can begin to work
with the thought or judgment and question its validity. We can
then ask ourselves: "Is it really hopeless? Did I really mess up?
Am I really a lost cause incapable of change? Is it true that I am
not a good person?"

The more you come to recognize the different ways the critic
takes root in us — physically, emotionally, and energetically —
the more likely you are to find strategies to counteract its impact

and begin to reclaim parts of yourself and your life that you had lost.

◄ PRACTICE ►

Reducing the Impact of Judgments

As you go through your day, try to sense the various effects that judgments are having on you. How do you feel emotionally, physically, and mentally when you are judging yourself?

Similarly, when you feel foggy brained, physically heavy, emotionally hopeless, or just plain bad, try to articulate what judgments might be fueling your feelings. (This might involve some guesswork.) Try to bring those judgments into the fresh light of day in your mind. Write them down in your journal if you wish.

Once you have a sense of what the judgments are or might be, begin to work with them analytically. Ask yourself these questions about each judgment:

- Is it true?
- What is it trying to say?
- What might lie beneath it?
- Can you see that it is just a point of view, not absolute truth?

Once you tease apart the thought from the emotional, physical, or mental state, notice whether you feel a sense of ease or clarity.

Put some space between yourself and the thought, as if you were observing it from a distance, like a cloud passing through the sky. Let the thought go, and shift your attention either to something more positive or simply to something happening in the present moment.

Sometimes, if the body is very heavy from the judgments, it's helpful to be more physical. You might try going outside, taking a walk, or doing some exercise to shift some of the heaviness.

CHAPTER FIFTEEN

IT'S ALL YOUR FAULT

Understanding the Critic in Relationships

If you judge people, you have no time to love them.

— MOTHER TERESA

Close relationships are one of the more common places for the critic to surface. The critical voices in our head first took root when we internalized attitudes and judgments from our family of origin and from the influential people around us. Not surprisingly then, the critic often shows up in our long-term relationships — not only with our spouses, but also with our parents, children, siblings, and friends. Relationships are also a place where we tend to project our critical thoughts onto others. Sometimes it then feels as if there are multiple critics we are living with both inside and outside.

Just as people often reserve their most personal and not-so-pretty selves for their loved ones, people also tend to allow the critic to unleash itself more on those they are closest to. Often with painful or even devastating results for themselves as well as their relationships.

I saw an example of this while teaching a course in a corporate setting. Jenny, a senior executive in a consulting company, noticed time and again how she needed approval from women she worked with, whether they were her seniors or not. She judged herself for that pattern, as she liked to think of herself as a successful, independent businesswoman who should be beyond approval seeking.

Though she did feel independent, she also felt needy at times and therefore vulnerable. As she began to mindfully inquire more deeply into these feelings, she realized they were coming from a deep need to be seen and approved of by her mother. She remembered a time when her mother took her aside as she was leaving home for college and said to her, "My husband has disappointed me. Your two older sisters have also failed me. But most of all you have disappointed me and let me down."

These parting words were excruciating for Jenny to hear as she was about to embark on a new stage in life. Her mother was disappointed because, instead of going into the sciences so she could become a physician like her father, Jenny was pursuing a bachelor's degree in fine art. This was the last of a long line of critical attacks from her mother that started in childhood.

Thirty years later she was still working with the impact of her mother's harsh words. However, once she realized there was part of her that was still a little girl inside, desperate for her mother's approval, she started (with a little bit of help and encouragement) to bring a kind attitude to that young, needy part of herself. Over time she slowly began to heal from those painful words and find her true autonomy. (You will learn how to cultivate this type of self-compassion in chapter 26.)

What was missing for Jenny's mother was not only some basic kindness, but an understanding of how great an impact one's words can have. What was also lacking was an understanding of the importance of accepting people as they are and letting them grow and unfold in the way they need to. How often do we insist that people be a certain way? How frequently do we criticize if others don't conform to our expectations, likes, or desires?

If acceptance is not available to us, then we will likely keep judging when we don't get what we want. Similarly, when others hurt us, commit a wrongdoing, mess up in some way, or let us down, how easy is it for the judge to criticize or condemn? We can hold on to such grudges for weeks, months, sometimes a lifetime.

Without forgiveness and the ability to acknowledge our own humanness and fallibility, the judge holds us and others to impossibly high moral standards. It can then be quite harsh with all those who do not live up to those standards, including ourselves.

To be clear, this is not about ignoring past hurts, denying painful things when they happen, or shying away from speaking up when necessary. It is about learning how to acknowledge difficult things when they happen, without getting lost in a tirade of judgments and righteous indignation.

Sometimes in relationships the critic can manifest in quite subtle ways yet still have a dramatic impact on our well-being. Jason, a graduate student in psychology, felt weighed down by the heaviness of his critic. He recounted how easily his critic got triggered by other people's comments. He talked about his last relationship, where his boyfriend was also quite critical of others.

Being in close quarters, he was often within firing range of his partner's judge. He talked about an incident that occurred when he came back from hiking on his day off and his partner made a seemingly harmless yet loaded comment. His partner remarked how lucky Jason was to have enough time to hike, given all the work that needed to be done around the house. That was followed by another apparently benign question about whether Jason had picked up the milk from the store on his way home. These comments landed quite differently than was perhaps intended. The impact of one's words and actions are often radically different from the intention behind them.

Despite the sense of expansiveness Jason was feeling after the hike, the questions hit at a strain of unworthiness in him. They touched a seam of guilt about the possibility that he was not pulling his weight, not doing his fair share around the house. His partner was sensitive to being taken for granted for doing the lion's share of the house chores. And his questions, though perhaps innocent, triggered Jason's own self-judgment.

Then Jason's clarity of spirit, which had come from his hike, evaporated. He was left with a sense of heaviness, as if his mind were quietly saying, "You are too self-centered, not considerate of others, and absentminded."

How easily the critic is triggered! And how careful and caring we need to be in relationships to avoid passing on our own critic, or our family's, to our loved ones. It's not that we can't critique, or discern what is and what is not working, but we do need to be mindful of the unconscious, emotionally laden judgments in our words and have an intention to speak and act with care and kindness. If we don't have such an intention or thoughtfulness, it is likely the critic's voice will keep seeping out into our communication with those close to us — in our tone, words, body language, and behavior — to the detriment of our relationships.

⟞ PRACTICE ⟝

Examining the Critic in Your Relationships

Look at your relationships with family, friends, and other loved ones, and notice how your critic operates when you are around others:

- Are your judgments frequent?
- What sparks the desire to judge those you are close to?
- What thoughts or feelings motivate the criticism?
- What is the intention behind voicing the criticism?
- When you are being critical, is the comment necessary (even if it's true)?
- How does it feel when you are critical of people close to you?
- Is there any righteousness in your judgments?
- Are your judgments a reenactment of judgments others made about you in the past?
- What impact do your judgments have on your sense of connection with the people around you?
- Do you hold people you care about to higher than usual (or impossibly high) standards?
- Are you less forgiving of those close to you?

As you start to pay more attention to the critic in relationships, you may see how judgments are happening unconsciously and how they can negatively impact those around you. Try not to let this be the basis for judging yourself, but let it inform your choice of what to say or not say.

PART THREE

HOW TO WORK MINDFULLY WITH THE CRITIC

CHAPTER SIXTEEN

MINDFULNESS

◄ ►

The Power of Awareness

Mindfulness is the aware, balanced acceptance of the present experience. It isn't more complicated than that. It is opening to or receiving the present moment, pleasant or unpleasant, just as it is, without either clinging to it or rejecting it.

— SYLVIA BOORSTEIN

If you haven't noticed, mindfulness is quite the buzz these days. It has been on the front page of *Time*, the *New York Times*, *Wired*, *Psychology Today*, and numerous other magazines. It has been featured on TV shows such as *Oprah* and *Dr. Oz*. CEOs, politicians, and athletes are claiming that it is what gives them a competitive advantage. Psychologists, doctors, and neuroscientists are studying its benefits for mental and physical health.

So what exactly is mindfulness? The simplest definition is "clear awareness." It is the capacity to be present, consciously knowing what is happening in your experience moment by moment. You can apply that attention to your mind, body, or environment. It is both a state of mind and a quality that you can develop through practice. Although we all have access to this quality, it takes patience and perseverance for it to become part of the fabric of who you are.

Now, as you read this, you may be thinking that you are already aware, that you already know what's going on. That may be true on one level. But if you take a closer look, you will see there are many times in the day when you are not fully present. If you have ever tried to concentrate on one thing in meditation, such as your breath, you know just how challenging it is to stay present for very long.

Take an ordinary activity like driving. How many times have you driven somewhere and been asked which way you came, only to realize you can't remember which streets you drove down? Of course, you had some modicum of attention because you didn't crash or get lost. But memory partly depends on attention, and if you are not mindful, not conscious of what is happening as it is happening, then you are probably on autopilot. This is one of the reasons we don't remember much.

Autopilot is what happens when we've done something, like walk, drive, or do the dishes, so many times we don't need to focus on it anymore with mindful attention. It almost does itself. So, as we're doing that activity, we start to space out or think about things like our to-do list or the top ten tunes of what's worrying us. Or we muse on what to cook for dinner, the problems in our relationship, or the terrible state of the world. Whatever it is, our attention is not on what we are doing. It is elsewhere.

This divided focus has been referred to as "constant partial attention." It is the multitasking brain, which allows us to do more than one thing at a time, mostly to our detriment. Often we choose to do this to get through all the demands of our busy day, whether it's looking after the kids while cleaning the kitchen, or commuting to work while taking a call from a client.

Sometimes our job demands it of us. Yet it leaves us not present to much of anything. We are on the phone, but also checking our email. We are reading an important document for work, but also listening to the news on the radio. We are at a dinner party, but also checking our smart phone for Facebook updates. Our kids are talking to us, but we are also figuring out a work problem.

The net result is that we are not very present, and that is the opposite of being mindful. I've seen funny but painful YouTube videos of people walking while texting — and banging into lamp-posts, tripping over curbs, falling down stairs, even bumping into a bear on the loose in a mountain town! I have seen cars driving out of the shopping mall with six-packs of beer left on the roof and coffee cups left on the trunk. How many times have you seen people look for a pair of glasses they were already wearing?

Perhaps we should be a little more alarmed at all of this inattention because of the harm it can cause, especially as we are all so consumed by our screens and devices. Texting while driving has become an epidemic. Nearly 330,000 injuries occur each year from accidents caused by texting while driving. The National Safety Council reports that cell phone use while driving leads to 1.6 million crashes each year.

Yet contrary to the popular myth that multitasking helps us get more done and be more efficient, research shows that multi-tasking on the job diminishes both our efficiency and the quality of our work. Even worse, multitasking releases the stress hor-mones cortisol and adrenaline, which can lead to all kinds of health problems.

A large study conducted by Harvard Medical School turned up some surprising results about the effects of not paying atten-tion. Researchers asked people in the study three questions as they went about their day: "What are you doing?," "Are you paying attention to it?," and "How do you feel?" They tracked several thousand people over a period of weeks, checking in on them by phone throughout the day and asking them those three questions.

They discovered that, on average, participants were not present 46.9 percent of the day. If we sleep for roughly a third of the day and are only present half of our waking hours, then by the time we are sixty, we've only been awake and present for twenty years! That's a lot of time lost.

What was perhaps more important in the findings was that people reported feeling happier when they were present, even if the activity was a mundane chore like laundry, washing dishes, or ironing. The study revealed that, again contrary to popular belief, people are not happier when they just space out or daydream during a dull activity. So next time you are cleaning the house, walking the dog, or taking a long drive in your car, give it your full attention and see for yourself what happens.

For the past decade mindfulness has been in the spotlight, with thousands of studies being conducted on it. Although the research is still preliminary, there is an emerging body of evidence that points to its potential benefits. It has been shown to improve attention, concentration, and learning; reduce stress and blood pressure; and enhance immunity and memory. Not bad for one quality of mind.

The good news is we all have an innate ability to be aware. It is the nature of our mind. However, most people's minds are untrained, so the way many of us use our attention is less than optimal. Just look at our dopamine-hungry habits of seeking novelty and stimulation when working on the computer. How often do we get seduced into web surfing, online shopping, or cruising Facebook or Snapchat while trying to focus on a work project? That inattention and quick task-switching then becomes its own habit, its own well-worn neural pathway that diminishes our concentration and effectiveness.

Another reason we are not so good at being present is that we are too caught up in distractions and often unable to just be with ourselves. In another study, participants were asked to sit in an empty room with no stimulation for fifteen minutes and do nothing except think. They could also choose to do that but, while in the room, administer unpleasant electric shocks to themselves. Interestingly, a large percentage of participants (up to 67 percent of men) chose to receive an electric shock rather than face the discomfort of no stimulation and being alone with themselves and their thoughts. One participant administered the electric shock over 180 times! What would you do in that situation?

What mindfulness brings to us in this attention-deficient, overstimulated culture is the ability to find a sense of grounding and focus amid the chaos of competing pulls on our attention. It trains us to be aware of those impulses toward distraction yet remain steady and not react to them.

If mindfulness is so helpful, then how do you start? A metaphor that is often used is one of training a puppy. You probably know that a two-month-old puppy is very exuberant and into everything — every sound, smell, stimulation, and chewable thing. Sound like someone you know? So you have to begin with learning to stay, just like a puppy — to stay steady in the present moment, no matter what else is going on.

The easiest way is perhaps one of the simplest and oldest techniques known to man, which is to focus your attention on the physical sensations of your breath and notice each time your mind wanders off in a different direction. You practice this a few billion times until your mind gets the hang of it, and staying present starts to take less effort. Once this has become easier, you begin to apply that focused attentiveness to everything else in your experience, to your whole life.

But how does this relate to the complexity of life? Perhaps the most relevant example is how it translates to our most common activity, looking at a screen, be it a computer, smart phone, or TV. With mindfulness you simply focus on the task at hand, like writing your college paper, crunching some numbers, programming, crafting a proposal, or reading a document, rather than leaping on every impulse to check the stock market, look on eBay for a bargain, or see if airline ticket prices have gone down for this summer's vacation.

Mindfulness brings awareness to what you are doing, and with that clarity comes the possibility of choice. You can learn to intercept unhelpful, unwanted habits and cultivate positive ones. And as you learn to do that in the laboratory of meditation, you can translate it to any activity, whether it's playing sports, writing computer code, or listening to your child when they come home from school.

⟞ PRACTICE ⟝
Cultivating Mindfulness

Mindfulness has been cultivated and practiced for thousands of years through the art and science of meditation. Think of meditation as a lab for the mind that produces awareness in a concentrated form.

This exercise is a meditation that will help you strengthen your capacity for awareness so that you can cultivate mindfulness in your daily life.

1. Find a place where you can be undisturbed for at least ten minutes. Sitting in a chair where you can be upright yet relaxed, assume a comfortable posture. Allow your body to be at ease.

2. Gently close your eyes and turn your attention

inward. Sense how your body feels in this moment. Mindfulness is a quality of attention that's allowing, inviting, curious about what is. So as you pay attention to your body, see if you can bring a quality of attention that's accepting and allowing of how things are in this moment.

3. Move your attention through your whole body, noticing where you may be holding any unnecessary tension, inviting your belly and shoulders to relax, softening the muscles around your eyes and face, relaxing your jaw.

4. Sit with awareness of your body, and notice that it is naturally breathing by itself, your breath effortlessly coming and going. Allow your breath to be exactly as it is, and bring your full attention to it. Notice how your breathing is in this moment. Is it long or short, deep or shallow, relaxed or tense? Notice how your breath changes each time you breathe.

5. Be with your breath as though you were encountering it for the first time, as if this were the first breath you ever took.

6. Notice where you feel your breath most clearly. Is it at the nostrils as the cool air enters and warm air leaves your nose? Or in the back of your throat? Or in the lifting and expanding of your upper chest when you inhale or the contraction of your chest when you exhale? Or perhaps in the rising and falling of your abdomen?

7. Establish your attention in the place where you feel your breath most clearly. Pay attention to the full duration of an in breath and an out breath.

Stay present if there's a pause between breaths; simply be aware of your body sitting until the next in breath comes. When you notice sounds appearing and disappearing, sensations arising and passing, emotions, thoughts, and images coming and going, just acknowledge them and then bring your attention back to your breath.

8. If it is helpful, you can make a soft mental note of "in" when you inhale and "out" when you exhale. Make sure the mental note takes only about 5 percent of your attention and that the majority of your focus is on feeling the actual sensations of your breath.

9. If your attention becomes absorbed in thoughts, memories, or plans, simply reestablish a connection with your breath. When you notice that thinking is happening, that itself is a moment of mindfulness. There is no need to judge yourself; just bring your attention back to your breath.

10. As a way of deepening your attention to your breath, focus on the very beginning of an in breath. Gently sustain your attention just for that one in breath. Then notice the beginning of an out breath, and sustain your attention just for that one out breath.

11. No matter how many times your attention wanders or how far you become lost in thought, it takes only a moment to return to mindfulness, to the present moment. Return to the present moment by reestablishing a connection with your body and then reconnecting with your breath.

12. It's natural for the mind to think. Mindfulness practice is coming into wise relationship with

thought and with everything that happens in your experience. So without judgment or criticism, bring your attention back again and reestablish a connection with your breath. Connect and sustain your attention with each in breath and each out breath. Notice how each breath is different from the previous one. Allow your awareness to be absorbed by and permeate each breath. Pay attention to the fine sensations and nuances of your changing breath. If you find yourself becoming tense or trying to control your breath, relax a little, making sure there's ease in your body.

13. In the last few minutes of the meditation, let go of what's gone on before and just begin again. Allow yourself to simply be aware of sitting and breathing. Rest in this natural awareness of your breath as it comes and goes.

14. As you begin to bring this meditation to a close, take a moment to sense your body, your heart, and your mind. Notice the effect of this exercise.

15. When you feel ready to end this meditation, slowly open your eyes, and gently move and stretch.

Bring the same quality of mindful attention you used in this meditation to everything you encounter. See if you can sustain this mindfulness as you move through your day. And remember that the more you do this formal mindfulness training, the more you'll be able to bring mindful awareness into the rest of your life.

CHAPTER SEVENTEEN

HELLO JUDGMENTS

Realizing Judgments Are Just Thoughts

Don't pay any attention to what they write about you. Just measure it in inches.

— ANDY WARHOL

M indfulness is an intentional quality of attention that provides clarity, awareness, and a sense of choice regarding what we pay attention to and the way we pay attention to it. It also supports us in sustaining our focus on the task at hand. When we turn that lens of attention toward ourselves, it can foster a clear self-awareness. It is this ability to know ourselves that is essential when dealing with the critic. Most of the time we don't notice the chatter that's always going on in our brain. We notice even less the chatter of our critical mind — it has become "part of the furniture."

The less we are aware of our judging thoughts, the more likely we are to let them chirp away, slowly eroding our sense of self-worth. Mindfulness helps you become acutely aware of your thoughts — the good, the bad, and the ugly, or as one person amusingly referred to their judge, "the itty, bitty, shitty committee." Without awareness there's no possibility of a different course of action. When we see the painfulness of our judgments clearly, we see that we have a choice, and we can begin to develop strategies to diminish their influence over us. This is one of the gifts of mindfulness.

Mindfulness is not just about paying attention; its role is to support understanding, insight, and greater well-being. How does it do this? It helps you discern what is healthy and helpful and what is not. And with that information you can decide on the best course of action. Do you keep letting the critic's negative voice drone on and on? Do you listen to it? Do you believe it or do what it tells you? With the ability to discern, you can choose to ignore the critic and shift your attention to something more constructive.

The foundational skill is the ability to differentiate between a thought that is judging and one that isn't. Mindfulness helps you examine your thought processes and discern what kinds of thoughts are occurring. Using this skill, you can begin to isolate the judgments from all the other thoughts. You can learn to feel it in the tone — if your mind is barking at you critically for forgetting something, it is a judging thought. If a thought is challenging your innate value, it is a judgment. If you are starting to feel weighed down by self-recrimination over a past decision, you can be sure the critic is at work.

Once you turn the lens of awareness toward your own mind, you may be surprised how many thoughts are actually judgments and how frequently they occur. It can be an informative and sometimes entertaining exercise to count all the judgments that occur in a day. When you get to 568 by lunchtime, you begin to realize how preposterous they all are, and it helps you not take them so seriously. Or, conversely, it is a wake-up call that spurs you to really do something about this judging habit.

At first this can feel a little depressing or overwhelming. As you practice and develop mindfulness, it sometimes seems like you are going backward because you see a whole host of thoughts you never knew you harbored. However, it is better that you are aware of them than not. Once they are within your awareness, you can transform them and break their power over you. Who doesn't want that?

Let me share an example of how this happens. I regularly teach at a meditation center called Spirit Rock. It is located in a beautiful, pastoral setting in the hills of Northern California. During a meditation retreat there, I was working with a student who was an actor and theater director from New York. This student, a woman in her forties, had a particularly loud and incessant inner critic.

All through the retreat, and similarly all through her life, she had been bombarded with self-judgment. She said it was just part of being an actor — you get used to it. Of course, you never really get used to an old curmudgeon living inside your head. It is always prickly and jarring. She did say that her critic made her life miserable, which made her acting career that much more difficult.

I'd been supporting her through the mindfulness retreat, and, as often happens in an intensive meditation course, the introspection amplified her critical thoughts to such a degree that they became deafening. Then one day, after cultivating mindfulness for the better part of a week, she had a breakthrough.

As she was walking down the hill to the meditation hall, her critic was on her case, nagging her the whole time for not being a good enough meditator. Then, in a moment of clear mindfulness, she saw the critic for what it was. She exclaimed to herself, and later to me, "The critic is just a bunch of thoughts! They are just a bunch of thoughts!"

Suddenly, as in *The Wizard of Oz*, the person behind the curtain was revealed. The emperor truly had no clothes. There was nothing more to the judgments than a collection of repetitive words cycling through her head — words that had been blown out of proportion and given far too much significance. She realized that by taking them to be true, she had given them the authority to decide her credibility as an actor and her value as a human being.

Now, it's not as if her critic then vanished overnight. It rarely does after a lifetime of chatting away in our head. But once we burst the balloon of belief in the validity of its rants and stop giving it authority over us, we can have a radically different relationship to it. We then have the space to see it for what it is — just a bunch of words. And so it was for the actor. She felt as if a heavy burden had suddenly been lifted from her shoulders, and she was able to distance herself from the critic enough to see herself more clearly. Peace of mind was now more within reach, at least for brief moments, and important foundations for freedom were being laid.

=== **PRACTICE** ===

Recognizing Your Judging Thoughts

The key to this practice is to distinguish the judging thoughts, especially the ones that are laden with negative emotions and put-downs, from all the other random thoughts that float through your brain.

There are many ways to learn to recognize the critical thoughts in your head. One simple way is to begin noting them with your awareness. Then, each time you notice you are judging yourself for something or being critical of others, use the following mindfulness technique:

Make a mental note by saying the word "judging" silently to yourself. This helps crystallize the understanding that you are judging and helps the judgment stand out against the backdrop of other thoughts.

If you notice that you judge the judging (or that you judge yourself for judging your judgments!), repeat the mental note "judging," being careful not to say it with a harsh or critical tone.

See the judging as simply a bunch of words that you have given particular weight to in the past.

You can also say "judgments are like this" as a way of acknowledging that this is just how judgments are.

As you become more attuned to your judging mind, notice whether this changes your relationship to the judgments in any way. Sometimes just shining the light of awareness on a mental process is enough to create some distance from it.

If the judging thoughts keep pulling you into their vortex, then as well as noting them, shift your attention to something that will allow you to stay present to something other than thoughts. For example, feel your breath, notice sounds, look around at something interesting or pleasing.

If seeing the extent of your judgments makes you feel demoralized or more critical, remember that whenever you become conscious of something, you have an opportunity to work with it. If you are not cognizant of it, there is no hope of transformation.

A slightly different but fun practice is to count your judgments every day for a week. Notice what happens when you see just how many there are. See if that also helps you detach from their stickiness and power.

CHAPTER EIGHTEEN

TEFLON MIND

◄ ►

The Power of Nonidentification

There is nothing either good or bad, but thinking makes it so.

— WILLIAM SHAKESPEARE

One of the greatest gifts of mindfulness is that it allows us to cultivate a Teflon mind. What does that mean, and how does it relate to us since it usually refers to cookware? Normally, our mind is like Velcro. Everything sticks. It is as if those judging thoughts come wrapped in hooks and barbs and lodge themselves in our mind each time they arise. The outcome is that our judging thoughts stay firmly entrenched, taking up residence in our mental attic and making it feel cluttered and full.

In contrast, mindful awareness creates a sense of space. When we bring awareness to something, it becomes enveloped in a spacious clarity, just as when we shine a light on something in the dark we see the object but also notice all the space around it. In the light of awareness, thoughts can be seen more clearly and lose their sticky quality. Awareness is like the sky, and from this perspective thoughts are just clouds passing through the sky. They don't stick to it. They float, they move. They don't obscure the sky.

Mindful awareness is essential for learning to not identify ourselves with our thoughts. This nonidentification means we no longer believe the thoughts or take on board what they are saying about us. We see they are just conditioned processes that are no more objectively true than anything else. Nonidentification allows us to detach, disengage, and not get caught.

When we experience our inner and outer world with awareness, we become like the conductor of an orchestra, aware of all the components that make up the symphony, but not caught up in any individual part. Or like a calm grandparent with a child who's throwing a tantrum — the child can yell, cry, kick, and scream, but the grandparent knows it will pass and so isn't ruffled by it.

The second essential factor that supports nonidentification is an understanding that what comes from the critic is, for the most part, neither accurate nor helpful. The more we examine the arguments of the critic, the more likely we are to detach from them. The more we understand there are much wiser, clearer, and kinder places within our psyche to turn to for clarity and advice, the less we will listen to, or even care at all about, what the critic has to say. Rarely does the critic offer anything that is original or that could not be ascertained from a more reliable source.

Another example of how nonidentification works can be seen in emotional reactivity. Think of a time when you were emotionally attached to a particular point of view in an argument. What happened when that point of view was challenged? You may have become emotionally reactive — defensive, swept up in anger, with a sense of righteous indignation. Sometimes in this kind of scenario, in the midst of your reaction, it may dawn on you that the other person's point of view is correct, or you may see the limitation of your own position. At that point, you dis-identify with your position for a moment, step out of your own way, and suddenly find more space, greater ease, and sometimes a tad of embarrassment at seeing how caught up you were. Again, it is the awareness, the knowing, that allows the disengaging to occur.

A similar process can happen when judgments arise. The more we look at them with mindful awareness, the more we can see them for what they are, and the more we are able to dis-identify with them. We come to see they are just thoughts, just points of view, each with its particular bias and limited perspective, often a very old and distorted one.

One of the things I encourage people to do when the critic is hurling judgments at them is to say, "Thank you for your opinion" or "Thanks for your point of view." There need not be defensiveness; you merely need to see the judgments for what they are — just a bunch of opinions, like a cluster of clouds in the sky. That allows you to let them go much more easily and to find space again. Then the judgments can fall from your mind without sticking, like rain against a windowpane.

One last crucial tool for cultivating the attitude of nonidentification is ceasing to take ownership of the thoughts, judgments, and criticisms. Mark Epstein, psychiatrist and meditator, titled one of his books *Thoughts without a Thinker*. He was pointing to an age-old philosophy that understands that thoughts think themselves, that there is no one behind the curtain pulling the strings, thinking the thoughts. The thoughts are happening by themselves, based on causes and conditions that bring them into existence.

Julie, an accountant in a course I was teaching at Esalen in Big Sur, reported struggling with her critic. She noticed that whenever she was doing her personal bookkeeping and the books didn't tally correctly, she was immediately judgmental of herself and her accounting skills. A critical thought was instantly triggered: "If you can't even manage your own accounts properly, how do you expect your clients to trust you with their books?" She says it was like an automated response. She had heard it countless times.

Did Julie think this thought? Did she will it into being or invite it in? Or did it happen by itself, triggered by her conditioning and layers of fears about needing to be accurate, and worries about her clients' reactions if she miscalculated? Doesn't the brain just do that automatically? Most judging thoughts just happen in this knee-jerk fashion, in the same way that the brain labels a stimulus "bird" when we hear a bird's morning song outside our window in spring. The more we see that thoughts think themselves, the less we need to feel the unnecessary burden of responsibility for our thoughts, and the more we can see them as an impersonal process that will continue to twitter, in the same way the birds will chirp outdoors.

It is precisely this process of not taking our thoughts so personally that makes nonidentification possible. We can see the judging thoughts from the perspective of a third-person observer and not feel so burdened by them. This is when we really begin to feel a sense of spacious ease and peace.

⟜ PRACTICE ⟞

Not Identifying with Your Judging Thoughts

For this practice you will do a reflective meditation. Try to do this practice outside — for example, while sitting or lying down on a hillside, on the beach, in a park, or in your backyard.

1. Gently close your eyes and visualize your mind as a vast, open, blue sky.
2. Now open your eyes and look up at the sky, and imagine or feel how your awareness can mingle

with that space so that you feel as vast as the space of the sky above you.

3. Imagine your thoughts are like clouds passing through that vast space of sky.

4. Now picture one of your recurring judging thoughts floating on a cloud above you. Focus on that cloud for a moment, and see if you feel any constriction, any narrowing of your perspective.

5. Notice how the sky holds the cloud-like thought without sticking to it, without being in the slightest way perturbed by it. See and feel the spacious sky all around the cloud. This is the space of awareness. Remember that even if a large storm cloud arrives, it only temporarily obscures the openness of the sky.

6. See the cloud that is carrying your judging thought drift away softly and notice again the vast sky.

7. When you feel ready to end this meditation, slowly open your eyes, and gently move and stretch.

See if this exercise helps you feel that quality of the Teflon mind, where the thoughts simply don't stick in the same way, where you reside merely in the knowing of the thoughts, in the awareness of them, rather than wrestling with them.

CHAPTER NINETEEN

KEEP IT IN THE FAMILY

◄ ►

Recognizing the Origins of the Critic

*Good judgment comes from experience, and a lot of that comes from
bad judgment.*

— WILL ROGERS

Did you ever wonder why the heck you have this critic in your
head? And, since it is so unpleasant, where did it come from
and why?

Usually, the critic represents the internalized voice of parents,
caregivers, and other influential people you had in your life when
you were growing up. The next time you notice your critic, examine its tone, language, concerns, and perspectives. Does it remind
you of someone? Or perhaps more than one person? We are not
doing this to cast blame for these voices from the past, but simply
to understand the source of the judge.

One client from New York I worked with shared a story from
her childhood that was particularly formative in this respect. Her
mother had been a figure-skating champion as a child. What came

with that success was an obsession about her weight and appearance. She also had strong ambitions for her daughter and hoped she would also become a similarly successful figure skater. My client remembered her mother being hypersensitive about her daughter's eating habits and hypercritical if she ate too much or started to put on even the slightest bit of weight.

Sadly, this ended up giving my client an eating disorder and left her with punishing judgments about food and her weight. Even though she did have a brief stint of success on the ice, she was unable to bear the internal stress and, after a breakdown, left the performing arts and became a psychologist to help others with similar challenges. She is still working with those voices in her head that were implanted by her mother. However, now that she is clearer about their origin, it is easier for her to see whose voices they are and to realize that she does not need to give them attention. They are her mother's issues, not hers.

So if you turn inside and listen, is your critic the voice of your mother, your father, your grandparents, your nanny? Sometimes it is the voice of a religious authority figure, such as a priest from your local church. Occasionally it is the voice of an overbearing schoolteacher. Sometimes it is the voice of an older sibling.

In adolescence the views and judgments of friends and classmates are often more important to us than those of our parents or family. The pressure to be liked, and to conform in terms of image, looks, physical prowess, and so on, is intense for teenagers. The relational experience in adolescence can be as formative for the personality as it is in early childhood. This in turn can flavor or generate different versions of the inner critic. So notice whether your critic is also influenced by voices from that period of life.

Once you recognize the origin of your critic's voice, you can see that it is not really your own, but something that has lodged itself in your mind over time. This can help you disengage and dis-identify from it a little more easily. Remember this voice was internalized at an early age. In order to survive your childhood, you had to toe the line to fit in, to maintain the flow of affection and love from your caregivers. So at that stage of life, without your inner critic, you ran the risk of a withdrawal of love and affection.

As you read this, you may have the thought that your parents were not that critical toward you or that you grew up as an atheist and there were no religious messages to internalize. So where did the critical voices come from? Children are sponges and soak up the atmosphere they are in. They often pick up the way parents treat themselves.

Jamie was a meditation student of mine and a successful physician. She had graduated from college early and had gone on to publish important research in the mental health field. She said she had grown up in a somewhat cold family. There was no hostility or outward criticism hurled her way. However, her parents were driven, and pushed themselves in their own medical careers. They were hard on themselves and were often critical of their own shortcomings.

The family values were to work hard and never let oneself off the hook, but to always try harder and never settle for second best. Sometimes she would hear her father berating himself for not excelling enough in his career. Her mother was always pointing out her own flaws as a parent while she juggled career and family. They had both come from immigrant families, and the culture of industriousness was carried to the point of self-harm.

So although she was never attacked with judgment, Jamie internalized this work ethic as well as her parents' habit of being hard on themselves. Even though she had a successful career, it was never enough, and her critic was as tireless as she was in her work. She would reproach herself when she took time off for herself, and vacations always needed to have a work focus. Even her days off were devoted to studying the latest research in her field. As successful as she was, it came at a price: she felt tight, hemmed in, and not free to enjoy the simple pleasures of life.

With mindfulness we can begin to unearth the source of some of our judging habits. We can hear the voices of our ancestors in them. We can have compassion for the generations who have passed down these harsh words or internalized them from their family systems or cultures. With awareness we can start to break this pattern of intergenerational wounding. We don't need to do it with blame. Compassion allows us to see the bigger picture — to see that it's not personal, that it's no one's fault. Yet we can take a stand and meet our hardened inner voices with clarity and firmness, without buying into the words and sentiments they convey.

⟹ PRACTICE ⟸

Identifying the Critic's Voice

This practice can be one of the most helpful pieces of work you can do with the critic. As soon as you hear the critical voice in your head, judging you or others, that is your cue to reflect on whose voice the critic resembles. Ask yourself the following questions:

- Are these statements or harsh tones the way you were sometimes talked to when you were growing up?
- Does the critical voice sound like your parents or other caregivers? Does it sound more like one parent or caregiver than another?
- Does it remind you of another family member, perhaps a sister or brother?

- Does it sound similar to any other influential person from your childhood, perhaps a religious authority figure, such as a priest, minister, or rabbi? Or maybe a teacher who had a special influence on you?
- Does your critic speak the way your parent or caregivers harshly or critically spoke to themselves?

Once you have ascertained to some extent whose voice the critic resembles, you can begin to think about what was of particular concern to them in regard to you. Perhaps your father was concerned about how you would support yourself and so was fixated on your getting good grades or a college education. Perhaps your mother was concerned about your shyness and so was pushing you to be more extroverted, in hopes that you would be less isolated. Both of those concerns may have created judgments about you that you internalized.

The more you understand the origins of your critic's voice, the easier it will be to realize it is not necessarily your own, but one you inherited, internalized, or borrowed. This in turn will make it easier to separate yourself and your identity from it.

CHAPTER TWENTY

THE JOKE IS ON YOU

—◁ ▷—

Seeing the Funny Side of the Critic

*Keep your sense of humor, my friend; if you don't have a sense of humor,
it just isn't funny anymore.*

— WAVY GRAVY

I n my workshops, I make a point of bringing humor and levity to the subject of the inner critic. A seminar on judgment can be a heavy thing, so a spirit of lightness and play helps cut the heaviness that is usually weighing down on people in the room.

I will often tell a story about how you can't win with the critic, as a way of pointing out the humor of it. For example, you might set the alarm for early in the morning because of some noble intention you have — maybe to meditate, go for a run, or do some chores before work. And when the alarm goes off, the critic, disguised as your life coach, whispers in your ear, "You know, it's early, and you're tired. And they say it's really important to get enough sleep." So you press the snooze button and hit the pillow for another hour.

Then, when you finally wake up, what happens? The critic gets on your case, this time not as a friendly coach, but as your inner tyrant: "Why didn't you get up when the alarm went off? How come you can't follow through on things? Why don't you ever do any exercise in the morning? You are never going to get in shape. Just another thing to add to your list of failures." You are doomed if you listen, doomed if you don't. You can't win. It is important to see how often, when it comes to the critic, it is a no-win situation. It will tell you to do one thing and then judge you in the next breath for doing that same thing. So it is helpful to see the humor in it. Otherwise it can be just too painful. With a bit of perspective it's easy to see how laughable this is. But when you believe it, it's plain misery.

Mindfulness provides the space in which to see the humor. If we are too close, too identified with the voice, we get caught up in the judgments and suffer unnecessarily. It is the space of awareness and nonidentification that gives us perspective to see the irony of our human condition. Just as comedians use humor to point out our foibles and quirks, we can do the same with our judge and point out its idiosyncrasies.

One of the ways I play with the critic is making a joke of my own not-so-perfect habits, which the critic would normally crucify me for. I don't have the best memory, especially when it comes to keeping track of physical stuff, like my keys or wallet. And, like many people, I often leave for an appointment with not quite enough time to be punctual. So there is often pressure for me to be able to quickly grab all the things I need, just before leaving the house. And when the inevitable happens and I can't find something I need to find fast, then instead of judging myself, I just say, "Mr. Mindfulness wins the day."

I poke fun at the fact that I'm a mindfulness teacher who sometimes is not aware where he left his checkbook. Not something people would expect if they believe that a mindfulness teacher should always be present! It is the same if I get lost, or forget something at the grocery store even if I had the thing written on my shopping list. "Mr. Mindfulness goes shopping," I say to myself with half a smile, which undercuts any sting from the critical remarks of the judge.

This is not to abdicate responsibility, stop finding ways to be more efficient, or avoid getting help with organizational skills. It is about not getting down on myself for the small things in life and the particular quirks of my nature that will most likely express themselves. Listening to all the demands of your critic and engaging in a never-ending quest to be perfect are not the solution. Instead you can transform your relationship to the critic, using all the tools at your disposal, including the secret weapon of humor.

Sometimes cartoons can be useful in helping us inject humor into our relationship to the critic. In one *New Yorker* cartoon, for instance, a woman is asking her husband in a somewhat derogatory way, "It was only one Nobel Prize you won, wasn't it, sweetheart?"

Similarly, in a comic strip called *Rhymes with Orange*, there is a cartoon titled "The Checklist to Feeling Pathetic." It depicts some of the ways we sadly and comically make ourselves feel terrible. In one caption it says, "Think of all the people you regularly disappoint." When I'm reciting the cartoon, I add "especially those who share your last name!" The last caption, my favorite, says, "Relive embarrassing and awful moments that occurred years ago." This is a common mental pastime and one that never leads to a happy ending, especially in the hands of the critic.

When we laugh, not only do we learn not to take the critic so seriously, but we also connect with others in our common humanity. We take the judgments less personally. We see that our mind is a little crazy and that it's okay if we hold it lightly.

⟞ PRACTICE ⟝

Finding Humor in the Critic

This practice will help you laugh at the critic, or at least find some humor in its relentless crazy comments.

I find that, to stop taking the critic so seriously, it helps to be playful and make things a little theatrical. For example, you could (as I do), imagine your critic as an old English judge, with a long gray wig, casting a weighty judgment on your case.

Another way to add a bit of levity is to exaggerate the judgments to the point of absurdity. Instead of just being a bad meditator because your mind wanders, as your critic reminds you on a daily basis, how about agreeing and going one step further: "Yes, and I am probably the worst meditator who has ever lived or ever will!" In the same way, rather than just letting the critic remind you of what a bad parent you are, why not add, "And I am perhaps the worst parent in the whole of human history." (Of course, this only works if you don't really believe you are the worst parent in history!)

Sarcasm is another form of humor you can employ to bring some levity to the judgments whirling around in your head. When my critic predictably surfaces because I have forgotten a good friend's birthday and tells me what a terrible person I am for doing so, I will often reply, "Oh, really? Thanks for that very useful piece of information" or "Might you have anything else of use to add?" Think up some sarcastic phrases or dry retorts, and see how effective they can be for disengaging from the judge and its critical barbs.

CHAPTER TWENTY-ONE

REALITY CHECK

◄ ►

Are Your Judgments Really True?

Don't believe everything you think.

— ANONYMOUS

The validity of all the things the critic says about you would rarely stand up under close scrutiny. An exercise I use in my inner critic courses is to have people write down their "top ten tunes" — their ten most common self-judgments. Usually, a bit of horror ripples through the room. People often exclaim, "You mean I actually have to bring those thoughts out into the light of day?!" Or they ask nervously, "What if people see them? What if someone is looking over my shoulder and sees all the shameful things I think about myself?"

I remind participants that what rumbles around and around in the tumble dryer of our head is a bunch of thoughts that we often don't have much clarity about. When we bring them into the light of day and write them down, we can perceive them with more clarity. We tend to bring more discernment to the written word than to the noises spinning in our head.

Often, when we read our judgments on paper, we notice how biased or distorted they are. With our more rational mind, we can observe that they are not accurate or portraying the whole story. We can see how petty and inconsequential many of them are. Writing them down brings some objectivity to what is normally a murky inner process.

Byron Katie is a renowned spiritual teacher from Southern California. One of the gifts she brings to her teaching is a specific technique for examining one's thoughts to see if they are really true. She asks people to reflect on four main questions about their thoughts, views, and assumptions:

1. Is this thought or belief true?
2. Can you know this thought or belief is really true?
3. How do you react when you believe this thought or belief? (Or: Can you think of one good reason for holding on to this thought or belief?)
4. Who or how would you be without this thought or belief?

These are four very important questions we can ask of any thought. It is particularly useful to apply this line of inquiry to our judging mind. In my courses, after I have asked people to write down their top ten judgments, I ask them to apply these four questions to each judgment.

In one workshop, I worked with a young man from the Bronx who had recently dropped out of his third year of college due to high stress. He also felt that his university studies were not relevant to many of the real challenges he faced as an African American man in a tough neighborhood. He had grown disenchanted with the academic system.

In an exercise on the critic, he had written as one of his top ten views, "I'm a bad person." He was carrying a lot of guilt because he was the first person in his extended family to get to college and his parents had worked really hard to scrape together enough money to get him to Columbia University.

So we walked through the four questions together, starting with "Is it true that you are a bad person?" I asked him to look honestly at the reality of his life, to let in the evidence that even though he had dropped out of school and let his family down, his life was full of expressions of his good nature. And as he took some time to reflect, he could see how he was at times generous, thoughtful, and caring. It was obvious to anyone around him what a kindhearted person he was.

Often we really do believe our judgments. We are convinced they are true. Even when we ask ourselves the second question — "How can you know it is really true?" — we can come up with a body of seeming evidence to prove it. If that is the case, then we need to go on to explore the next two questions. Though sometimes when we really dig deep into the second question, we realize we cannot know for sure if views like "I am a bad person" are *really* true.

So when the student looked at the question "What do you get for holding on to this belief?," he got to see that by believing he was a bad person, he felt small, ashamed, and unworthy of his family's hard-earned money. Not much of a payoff — sounds like a recipe for unhappiness. It reinforced an old idea that he would never succeed because he was unable to follow through on things.

And when asked who he would be without that thought, he started to let in the possibility of being free from it. He imagined experiencing himself as lighter, as someone who is listening to his intuition about what he needs to do with his life and not being burdened by familial guilt and self-induced pressure. He opened to the possibility that he could make difficult decisions that would profoundly disappoint people he loves yet still be a good person, worthy of love.

Just walking through this process does not necessarily make our burdensome judgments disappear. However, it is not until we look at the negative result of our judging thoughts and beliefs that we begin to see their destructiveness. And when we imagine our life free of these negative views, it can give us more fuel to release their hold on us and discover what is really true.

What ideas or beliefs are you holding about yourself that go unquestioned? The problem with not inquiring into them is that they become a solid part of your identity, part of who you take yourself to be. Then the trouble begins when you start to live life in accordance with them. If all you can hear is the mantra that you are disorganized and cannot get your life together, then you will most likely make that happen by sabotaging efficiency and organization.

For a long time I carried a view that I was not organized in my business. I have always had multiple streams of work as a sole proprietor. So I have to juggle many projects, which is made more challenging by the fact that I travel a lot for work and often teach in different countries. Naturally, there are some loose threads, and balls that get dropped here and there. At one point I hired a consultant to give me feedback about my overall business to see if it could be more streamlined and I could be more efficient in it.

Much to my surprise, and contrary to my expectation that she would give me an F grade for organization, she observed that I had to be highly organized to keep so many streams of work functioning well and that I just needed to stop sweating the small stuff. However, my distorted self-perception focused mainly on all the details that were not going smoothly. So my mind maintained the view that I was disorganized, which kept me feeling small and incapable.

Sometimes we hang on to our old identities and stories even if they are painful. We often prefer to do that rather than adjusting to the present reality, which may be quite different, because it can be unsettling to change old ways. Our ego holds on for dear life to the familiar because it feels safe with what is known. Any change will require a letting go, a mini death, a release of an old identity, and an inner reorganization. From the vantage point of the ego, this can feel daunting. But when we feel the freedom that comes from releasing old views and judgments that have created pain, we are motivated to live more in accord with reality rather than with what our critic tells us is true.

━ PRACTICE ━

Questioning the Critic's Views

Begin by writing out a list of your top five or ten self-judgments. Then for each judgment, go through each of the four questions below, writing out your responses.

1. Is this judgment or belief true?
2. How can you know this judgment or belief is really true?
3. What do you get for holding on to this judgment or belief? (Or: Can you think of one good reason for holding on to this judgment or belief?)
4. Who or how would you be without this judgment or belief?

Once you have gone through the questions with some of your judgments, notice what happens internally. What is

your experience like when you begin to question and challenge the judgments?

You can continue this reflection process each time you
are harangued by a painful self-judgment. You may only
need to use one or two of the questions — sometimes the
question "Is this judgment true?" is enough. The more you
question the validity of the critic's judgments, the more you
will undermine its previously unchallenged strength.

This process is not necessarily about creating new views.
It is about questioning the faulty ideas and beliefs long held
in your mind by the critic. Inner peace comes from seeing
that you cannot be defined by stories, views, or negative
thoughts about yourself. The more you release the burden of
painful self-judgments that are no longer relevant, the more
accessible inner peace will be.

CHAPTER TWENTY-TWO

SORRY, I'M NOT INTERESTED

◄ ►

Living with Disinterest in the Critic

The mind is its own place, and in itself can make a Heav'n of Hell, a Hell of Heav'n.

— JOHN MILTON, *Paradise Lost*

I n my work with people over the years, I've always found it startling when I encounter people relatively free from the curse of
the judging mind. They definitely stand out in the crowd. There is
a lightness about them, which is as refreshing as it is rare.

A characteristic they share is not being bothered by the voice
of the critic. The words fall from their minds like water off a
duck's back. There is an indifference, and often an immunity, to
the impact of its words.

The fruit of that quality is resilience. They are more able to
bounce back from setbacks, which they experience not as failures,
problems, or deficiencies, but as temporary obstacles to overcome. They tend to approach the challenges of life with a can-do
attitude, and if they don't succeed, they are not burdened by the
assaults of the critic.

Their not being impacted by the critic is often accompanied by an optimistic bias in their view of the world and, particularly, of themselves. They have created fewer neural pathways focusing on the negative. Instead their mind more easily falls into the slip-stream of the positive, whether it is about themselves, others, life, or the projects they are working on.

So how do we go about becoming more indifferent to the crit-ic's words? The main thing is to realize there is not much value in what it is saying. There is nothing in its judgments that could not be discovered through our own discernment, inquiry, and con-science. Its judgments come in such a painful form that even if there were a grain of truth or usefulness in them, that value would be outweighed by the negative impact of its harsh delivery and what it implies about our self-worth.

Once we understand this, it becomes easier not to pay much attention to the critic's words. We can learn to hear it as back-ground static, like distortion on the radio. We can stop giving it the time of day.

One doorway into realizing the futility of listening to its words is seeing how predictable the critic is. How it is formulaic, almost scripted. The more we see that, the less we are pulled into listening to its disparaging comments.

I coach a university professor from California. As a specialist in immunology, he is frequently asked to lecture to government agencies on the latest developments in the field. Generally, he is a good and well-liked presenter. He feels confident about what he speaks on and enjoys the process.

However, when he feels like he "messes up" in a lecture, such as when he forgets some data, incorrectly references a scientific study, or doesn't have an answer at his fingertips, his critic revs up. This is even more pronounced when he has made an error in his slide deck for everyone to see.

Because he has been lecturing for over twenty years, he is very familiar with this process. He has done good work deconstructing his critic in our sessions and now feels he has a healthy handle on it. He knows that in the moment or right after the lecture, his judge will pick through every slipped word, every less-than-smooth transition, every question imperfectly answered. He is ready for the blast.

He can now distance himself from his critic's voice much more than when it first started happening. He now listens to the judge harping on as if it were the sound of distant traffic, just a noise in his head. He realizes he doesn't have to give much attention to it. Just a nonchalant and somewhat dry "Aha, there you are. Thanks for your point of view." That seems to be enough to defuse the potency of the judgment. At other times he may not even do that, but may just ignore the critic's radio broadcast.

It is helpful to be familiar with the usual cues, to know what prompts the critic to attack. Often it is when we are feeling scared or vulnerable or fearful of some kind of reprisal for "messing up." Knowing this, we can anticipate when it is going to unload some judgments. We can attend to the vulnerability or fear with care and at the same time we can then practice being less interested in what it has to say and think of it as a politician on the TV news who is all riled up about something. If we are not interested in their political perspective, we can just let the words wash over us.

⟹ PRACTICE ⟸

Cultivating Disinterest in the Critic

You can train yourself to be uninterested in the critic's words. Learning to ignore them will take time, though, given how much attention you have paid to them in the past.

Anytime you notice the critic judging you, practice seeing its words as clouds passing in the sky, or as the hum of traffic in the city, or like an old song going around and around in your head. You can know the critic's voice is there in the background but not give it the time of day. This requires you to shift your attention to something else, in the foreground. Turn your awareness to something physical or sensory that is happening in the present, internally or externally. Take time to savor anything that is uplifting or pleasant. Notice what happens in your body, heart, and mind when you do so.

Another technique you can use when you hear the critic's voice is to respond with a quick retort. One of my more common responses to my critic is "Oh please." This phrase comes out of me in a disinterested tone, as if someone is telling me something that I've heard fifty times before and that is boring and repetitive, which of course the critic is. This retort plainly shows I am not interested and would rather give my attention to something else. So try to find a response — some words, a phrase, or a mantra — that allows you to reply quickly to the critic while ignoring its judgment and shifting your attention to something more useful or satisfying.

PART FOUR

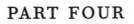

THE POWER
OF LOVE

CHAPTER TWENTY-THREE

BEFRIENDING YOURSELF

◄ ►

You Are Not Your Enemy

Be yourself — everyone else is already taken.

— OSCAR WILDE

The shift from living with attachment to the judgmental mind to living with kindness is perhaps the most important part of our work with the critic. It requires us to embrace all of who we are — the good, the bad, and the ugly. This can require a radical shift in our inner world, to allow ourselves to welcome into our heart the parts of ourselves we have denied, repressed, or rejected.

Carl Jung wrote, "One does not become enlightened by imagining figures of light, but by making the darkness conscious. The latter procedure, however, is disagreeable and therefore not popular." We can try running to the light for a while, as happens in a spiritual search, in the hope of bypassing all of the difficult, painful stuff of life. But that ultimately does not work. Genuine spiritual growth has to include all of who we are.

Fortunately, life has a way of encouraging us to deal with our disowned parts and hidden selves. In all of life there is a yearning for integration. At some point it is not a choice. Life will eventually grab us by the tail or slap us in the face to wake us up. It does that by finding ways to help us see the pain of splitting off vital parts of ourselves that we have denied. That certainly is what happened to me.

In my own spiritual journey, like many young, idealistic seekers, I had a skewed vision of what enlightenment was. It was a place that was far above the muck of everyday life. It was beyond the messiness of emotional pain and the conflicts of relationships. I wanted to transcend, to get above it all, so the challenge of being human wouldn't hurt so much.

Eastern meditative traditions seemed to offer a way out. I was on a fast track in meditation, heading only toward the light. I wanted to awaken so I could rise above the inner struggles. I didn't see then that I was misdirected in my search, driven by an unconscious fleeing from pain.

Such a naive aspiration has within it an inability to turn toward our more vulnerable, tender, and wounded places. But in the journey toward healing the pain of the inner critic, the essential transformation occurs when we begin to turn toward ourselves with kindness. That turn allows us to hold the pain of our losses, fears, and vulnerability as we would tend to a friend in distress.

Sometimes the urgency to transcend, to go toward the light, is itself an indication of the strength of the unaddressed pain that is waiting patiently to be healed. I see this frequently in my meditation courses. When I see that intensity of seeking, I often wonder what challenge or trauma may lie underneath the drive to transcend.

For most of my life I was quite unaware of the layers of trauma and wounds that I carried. There were parts of myself that felt incredibly tender and sad. Parts of my heart were frozen in fear, isolation, and numbness. Yet the more I opened to the spiritual path, the wider the chasm grew between the clarity and light I sought and the hurting places inside. The critic was my reminder, an indication that all was not well, a manifestation of how I had turned against myself. My search for the light was a defense against the sadness and pain within.

What the journey required was for me to stop trying to escape. I needed to find integration and wholeness right here, in my own body, inside my own skin. The peace I was looking for was not to be found in some heavenly realm, or in some rapturous mystical experience, but in a loving acceptance of the whole of my being. And that is the journey of descent, of journeying into the heart. We must be willing to be with whatever we discover there and hold it with love, acceptance, and tenderness.

The critic, for all its trying, does not know how to relate to those raw, wounded places inside except through fear and judgment. Generally, those painful inner parts of us were not so welcome by our family, friends, or society. We were often told we were weak for having such feelings. We were led to believe we were self-indulgent or self-pitying if we talked about them or gave them attention. We learned how to hide those emotions and put on a brave face, and we compensated in ways that others wouldn't detect.

When we do this, the critic tries to ensure we don't reveal any vulnerability that could open us to being hurt or exploited, so it shuts down the feelings with harsh, shaming words. This habit becomes second nature, and as we grow up, we get further and further away from the tender, raw places inside. And though they remain hidden, they continue to exert a powerful influence over our behavior.

I have worked with successful, well-known public figures who lived with this split. Outwardly, they were charming, gregarious, and successful in their field. Inside they held vulnerabilities, fears, and self-doubts. They were often ashamed of certain feelings that had lingered from childhood. They frequently displayed an intolerance toward being sensitive and caring toward the places inside that were hurting. They would judge themselves or these aspects of their character harshly. They would often say they wanted just to get rid of this inner stuff that was uncomfortable and move on. Sometimes their very success was a reaction to pain from their early life.

Why had they come to work with me if they were so successful? It turns out that the more they denied and pushed these parts of themselves away, the more they felt split inside. The outer triumphs began to feel more hollow when they realized it was hard for them to be with themselves in the quiet confines of their home.

What did all those accomplishments mean when they felt they couldn't be at peace in their own company? They were unable to tolerate painful feelings and could only view and judge them with meanness, which created an inner battlefield. It left a vast emptiness inside that they were desperately trying to run from.

Ted is a brilliant neurosurgeon from Vermont. He has everything in his life that you could imagine. He has a beautiful family, three healthy girls, and a highly successful private medical practice, and is a leader in his field. Yet when alone, he feels lonely and sad. In our work we explore the intense feelings he still has that linger from when he was young and tragically lost both parents in a car accident. He felt incredibly abandoned, lost, and alone.

After flunking in school for a time and being on the receiving end of a lot of pity and assumptions that his life was now fatally flawed, he decided to prove the naysayers wrong. He resolved to show them he was tough and could make it on his own. He hardened up, buckled down at school, and outshined his peers academically. When any sliver of the sadness crept in, he would shove it down by working harder, and shame himself for being weak.

Yet as he began to wake up to the chasm inside that had been held in by fear and the critic, he slowly began to integrate the pain from those losses. He realized he didn't need to turn away or resort to self-judgment.

He understood that he no longer needed to run from himself, and instead turned kindly toward those younger parts of himself that felt alone and abandoned. He saw how he continued the sense of abandonment by neglecting and ignoring his own needs. He began to release the incessant search for external rewards and validation that he had used to cover up the inner emptiness. He began to take on fewer projects and find some inner peace with who and where he was.

Life encourages us to live with integrity, wholeness, and honesty. To live out of alignment with those things is inherently painful. It is reality's way of making us live in harmony with its universal laws, because when we don't, we suffer.

And so, if we want to be free of pain, we must begin the important journey of integration, where we start to befriend ourselves. Where we turn toward our fears, pain, and insecurities with kindness rather than persecution and punishment from the judge. We can learn to distance ourselves from our critic so we can listen with sensitivity to these difficult parts of ourselves and hold them with tenderness.

A healthy milestone on this journey of integration is when we befriend our own pain as much as we do with our loved ones. The result is that we are able to be there for ourselves with compassion as we struggle, to be our own best friend when we are in the emotional trenches. This is not necessarily an easy thing. It takes patience and courage to keep turning toward those difficult places inside and to not slip into judgment, rejection, or shame. It also requires keeping the critic at bay with a firm compassionate strength that allows it no room to interfere with the process. No room to make us feel ashamed or weak. We do this with the understanding that to allow such tender, raw feelings to emerge, we need inner distance from the judging mind.

➤ PRACTICE ➤
Healing Your Inner Wounds

The poet Rumi, in his well-known poem referring to the human heart as a guest house, writes:

> This being human is a guest house.
> Every morning a new arrival.
> A joy, a depression, a meanness
> some momentary awareness comes
> As an unexpected visitor
>
> Welcome and entertain them all
> Even if they are a crowd of sorrows,
> who violently sweep your house empty of its furniture
> still treat each guest honorably...
> The dark thought, the shame, the malice...
> meet them at the door laughing
> and invite them in.

What would it be like to welcome any and all of your painful emotions, as Rumi suggests? What would it take to make that shift from turning away to embracing whatever lies there inside your body and heart? The following meditation will help you explore that.

1. Find a place where you can be undisturbed for at least ten minutes. Sitting in a chair where you can be upright yet relaxed, assume a comfortable posture.

2. Gently close your eyes and turn your attention to the sensations of your body and breath.

3. Once you feel settled and present, take some time to inquire into a hurt or difficult emotion you may be carrying from the past. Call to mind any childhood, adolescent, or recent painful burden within you. Stay attuned to your heart and body. Feel into any emotion that may be present.

4. Notice whether you have a tendency to turn away from yourself when you feel the pain, vulnerability, or sadness you carry. Instead of feeling the pain, do you get lost in thoughts or distractions?

5. As you connect with a painful memory or emotion, take a moment to say, "Welcome," and really let in the feelings. Experience them with a kind attention.

6. Notice any judgmental thoughts or reactions you have to those feelings. You can tell your critic in a firm but kind way that you are not going to listen to its comments, that you are going to create inner space to feel what lies beneath the surface.

7. If the feeling is intense, take long, slow, deep breaths and see if you can simply be with yourself in this vulnerable place. If the feelings that come up are too strong, shift your attention to something neutral like your breath, or sounds, until you feel grounded again.

8. Notice any agitation, restlessness, or desire to escape or to get lost in thinking. If that happens, bring your kind, soft attention back to whatever feeling is present, again and again. The more you settle into the tender feelings, the more you allow some resolution through your loving presence.

9. Keep bringing a kind, caring attention to these difficult emotions. You may even verbalize this in words that express your care or love, such as "May I hold my pain with kindness," "May I love myself just as I am," or "May I be free from pain."

10. When you feel ready to end this meditation, slowly open your eyes, and gently move and stretch.

Notice how you feel after doing this practice. Sometimes it is not easy to sit with our suffering. Yet even the intention to do so can allow a softening or opening toward the pain that lies within, and perhaps some understanding of it.

As you go about your day, try bringing this same kind attention to your emotions each time you feel vulnerable or in pain. Remember that you can practice this anytime you feel strong or difficult emotions starting to arise. Also remember that healing takes time, patience, and a lot of loving presence.

If this exercise resonates with you, you may also wish to use the RAIN practice in the last chapter, The Critic Toolbox, of this book to explore painful feelings.

CHAPTER TWENTY-FOUR

THE POWER OF VULNERABILITY

◄ ►

The Hidden Strength of the Heart

Butterflies can't see their wings. They can't see how truly beautiful they are, but everyone else can. People are like that as well.

— NAYA RIVERA

I often feel humbled by the critic. In the same way that I have practiced mindfulness and am still humbled when I sometimes forget where I parked my car in a parking garage. Despite all my time working with the critic, it can still get under my skin at times. It can still trigger a feeling of unworthiness that creeps in like mist, still attack me for the slightest thing, sometimes as a defense against feeling vulnerable.

I remember being under assault by the critic many years ago after a long period of the critic being quiet. It is hard to say what sparked it. Sometimes those waves come out of the blue. This time I was feeling particularly challenged by the administration of my various work projects, and I'd lost some money in a business transaction. Because of the workload and stress, I'd neglected some friendships, and my relationship was suffering. It felt like many details of life were falling through the cracks.

At times, when the judgments seemed to be endless, my spirits got very low. It felt as if everything I did was never enough. What kept this process in place was my being more allied with the critic than with myself. I would side with its harsh attacks. "Why can't I get my stuff together? Why am I letting people down and losing money?" its voice would rant. I thought its point of view seemed justified.

A natural reaction to such pain is to harden, to close down, to brace and contract, rather than feel. That is pretty natural, given how much it hurts. The problem with this attitude is that it keeps everything in check, and we freeze emotionally. It fails to provide the resources to deal effectively with those critical voices in our head or the emotional burden they inflict. It puts the process on hold, and it can drag on and on.

At some point I cracked open to feel just how painful it was to have lived under that critic's shaming voice. I also felt humbled that it had gone on for so long and that it was still having an impact. You could say the critic was judging me for not having done a better job at working on it! The net effect was that I felt raw and exposed.

This feeling of rawness is key to working with vulnerability. They often feel like one and the same thing. The challenge is to find a way to be comfortable feeling the innate vulnerability of being human. If we can hold our vulnerability with a loving attention, the painful feelings can unfold and slowly move through us.

In working with the critic, it is essential to shift our allegiance from the judge to ourselves. And just as we would do for a friend, we need to take care of ourselves and hold our own hand through these difficult, painful feelings. We must meet our pain with a kind heart, with a loving embrace as if we were holding in our arms a loved one who was hurting. It is the appropriate response when we are feeling battered with judgments. One of my teaching colleagues, Sylvia Boorstein, was able to model this in the way she would talk to herself when struggling. She would say, "Oh honey, you are startled. That's so hard. How can we help you? What do you need?" We can usually do that with others. The trick is learning to give that gift to ourselves.

Being with our pain in an undefended way can allow the healing quality of compassion to arise. Compassion is the heart's natural, caring response to pain. It is from the vantage point of the caring heart that we learn how to hold ourselves kindly. It is this same heartfelt attitude that strengthens our ability to defend ourselves. It is not an aggressive defense; it is a grounded, vulnerable strength that will not tolerate any harm to ourselves or others.

Fierce compassion says to the critic, "No, please don't talk to me like that. That is not helpful — it is hurtful." This quiet strength is an expression of our wise heart that will take care of us at any cost and will not let anything harm us. It is the strength of a mother bear. It is an attitude that replies to the critic, "I know you are trying to help, but it's not working. It's okay — I can take care of myself now. You can be quiet now."

I recall, during this difficult period, running late for an appointment, when I also realized I had double-booked myself and was not going to have as much time as I'd planned for either appointment. Then my car battery died between appointments, which meant I would be late for a public talk that evening. I could feel the tidal wave of judgment brewing for messing up my scheduling for the day.

Then something radical happened. Something softened inside, and instead of attacking myself with criticism, I just felt how hard it was to keep juggling such a packed client schedule, navigate unpredictable work circumstances, and try to manage an overly complex teaching life, all while doing a lot of business travel overseas. I felt the pain of that constant struggle to hold it together. And, out of the blue, a kind voice emerged that simply said, "Oh, this is hard for you. This is not easy for you, to manage your time and your life like this."

Those simple statements emerged after I'd done a lot of work on shifting allegiance away from my critic and on accepting the reality of my life and my challenges in dealing with it. This was not letting myself off the hook; it was just lovingly acknowledging to myself how hard I found it at times. It was letting myself feel the vulnerability of the situation, not listening to the critic, and feeling the pain of it. Once that occurred, it was easy to take the next steps of rearranging my calendar, calling roadside assistance for my car, and taking care of business without persecuting myself. It was a heartfelt, liberating moment.

For me the ability to access this self-compassion signaled a significant shift that allowed me to move from paying attention to the words of the critic to feeling the pain they inflicted. Since that time, there is no longer a cell in my body that wants to let such thoughts in. There is a quiet strength in the ability to rest in that tender place. Vulnerable it is; weak it is not.

It reminds me of a quote from the ancient texts that says, "Make your heart as vast as space, so big that nothing can harm it." When our hearts are that wide, it is as if the judgments are ripples on water, flowing away and leaving no trace. This is what vulnerability makes possible. It allows the natural strength of the heart to emerge.

⟶ PRACTICE ⟵
Opening Yourself to Vulnerability

The next time you find yourself being self-critical, take some time to register how that lands in your heart. Reflect on these questions:

- Can you feel the impact of those harsh words?
- Do you feel the residue of those judgments in your body?
- How does it feel to talk to yourself this way?
- What is the emotional repercussion of the judgments?

When you open yourself this way, see if you can let your heart be soft so you feel the tenderness that comes from feeling the pain of self-judgment. Vulnerability comes with opening the heart to feel the impact of the critic. But you are not opening it to let in someone abusive. You are merely opening your heart so you can feel the full impact of the ways you talk to or mistreat yourself.

Can you also let yourself feel the pain of the situation from which the critic is emerging? Ask yourself the following questions:

- Are you being berated for feeling vulnerable, weak, insecure, or deficient?
- Are you being attacked for a habit or personality quirk that you didn't intentionally choose to have?
- Are you being ridiculed for feeling vulnerable or for experiencing difficult emotions?

- Are you being judged for your personal challenges in managing your family and all the competing demands of your life?

Take some time to feel the pain of all those experiences.
None of them are easy to have or deal with. Can you feel
that these things are not your fault, just some of the burden
you carry in this life? Can you see how softening into the
vulnerability of your human condition can take the sting out
of being judged for your challenges?

From this soft but strong place, try to sense the voice that
lovingly but firmly says "No" to the way you let yourself
be attacked by judgments. Find that compassionate strength
that cares for you or the parts of your psyche that feel young,
vulnerable, or overwhelmed. When you do, you are less
likely to feel like a victim. Instead you can begin the slow but
important work of self-protection and empowerment.

CHAPTER TWENTY-FIVE

THE POWER OF LOVE

━◀ ▶━

Turning from Self-Hatred to Self-Kindness

We are people who need to love, because love
is the soul's life, love is simply creation's
greatest joy.

— HAFIZ

Love is perhaps the single unifying principle of all world reli-
gions. Every philosophy and spiritual tradition acknowledges
the centrality of cultivating love. What has stood out in my thirty
years of studying meditation is the necessity of cultivating love
for oneself as the basis for being able to fully love another. Without that, love is a pale reflection of itself.

Growing up as a Catholic, I always appreciated the message
of Jesus to love unconditionally. It is a beautiful teaching. Yet I
felt starved of an explanation of how to actually do that. How was
I to love my neighbors, I asked my mother in Bible study, when I
didn't like them or want to be near them! How was I supposed to
love the person that the priest was telling me was evil?

Among the things I have appreciated about the pragmatic teachings of the Buddha are his simple, practical instructions on how to cultivate the boundless heart of love. That there were techniques and methodologies to do this was a revelation to me. The primary way to do this is through loving-kindness meditation, or what is known as "metta" practice.

One translation of the word *metta* is "friendliness." This refers to befriending ourselves and everyone we meet, with a welcoming, nonjudgmental attitude. Now, of course, this is a practice, and most of us don't start out on the path with a very cultivated heart. When we begin, our heart has limits and constraints on who it loves and who it thinks is worthy of our affection. Usually it is restricted to a few near and dear folks. Rarely do we extend that warm, friendly affection to strangers, let alone ourselves.

The loving-kindness meditation practice begins with extending kindness and love to yourself, holding yourself with an attitude of friendliness and care. This is the hardest part for many people. This is particularly true if we have had a lifetime of listening to judgments berating us and reminding us of all the reasons we are not a good person, not doing enough, and not worthy of being loved. Yet in all my years of working with people, I've found this to be the most important place to start and the most radical antidote to the critic.

One of the reasons the kindness meditation is so potent in counteracting the critic is that it uses language (words, phrases, and wishes), the same medium the judge uses. Instead of listing all the things that are wrong with us and all the things we have failed at, we examine our deepest aspiration for ourselves. Then we put that wish into words, in the form of phrases that express our kind intention. We offer ourselves kind words like "May I be happy, safe, peaceful, and free." Then we repeat these words slowly and genuinely, letting them reverberate and ripple through our mind and body.

Over time, this creates new neural pathways, new synaptic connections. We literally rewire our brain so we don't fall into the same well-worn grooves of negative judgment. I see for myself how I have had a propensity to fall into a habit of self-criticism, yet the kindness practice has, over time, supplanted that habit.

So whereas once I would have chastised myself for being stressed out, the inner voice, trained by kindness, overrides the judgment and responds with kindness. "Oh," it says. "This is hard for you. Why don't you take some time to slow down, breathe, and see what other response is possible." And through this practice, I can see that kindness also has wisdom within it. It actually allows us to be more effective, respond better, and not drown in our reactivity.

Another way we cultivate love for ourselves is through our attitude. With mindfulness we can turn our attention to anything. When awareness is imbued with kindness, it is a powerful combination that gives us the capacity to be with anything. It is both clear and embracing, both present and loving. It is the type of attention we would bring to a child who is in distress. We would simply be with them with a caring presence, perhaps offering soothing words, but mostly just showing them we are there in a loving, present way. When we turn that quality of kind attention toward ourselves, it is a loving presence that can transform even the deepest self-hatred.

Joanna's story is a testament to what can happen when we turn this kind presence inward. During a snowy loving-kindness retreat in Canada, Joanna told me in a meeting how her heart felt frozen, as if there had been a hard stone living there for years. She said she was unable to do the kindness meditation. She felt numb during the long hours of meditation and wanted to leave.

As I do with many students, I invited her to do a guided, body-centered inquiry as a way to work more intimately with what was happening in her experience. She was a gardener, and when I asked her to feel the hardness in her heart, she said it was like a knot or a large, hard walnut. I then asked her to breathe into that space and to let herself feel any feelings that were there. She sensed sadness and numbness. I asked her to take her time during the course, to feel into the hard nut in her heart and be present with it, with a kind attentiveness, and then come back in a few days to check in.

When she returned, she talked about how she spent time feeling the hardness in her chest, but instead of freezing around it, she had embraced it with a warm loving-kindness rather than judging herself or criticizing it as wrong or bad. She had given herself time to feel the grief that was under the sadness, and the pain of being so shut out of her own heart. The pain of a lifetime of self-rejection and not being kind to herself began to dissolve.

As she was talking, tears were falling down her face. She said the tears were like kind rain that was melting the hard shell of the walnut and a small, tender shoot had started to grow from the nut. The beginning of a new life. It was clear from looking at her that this integration left her more full, bright, and whole.

Of course, this was only the beginning. But as a gardener, she knew she had done the important foundational work. She had prepared the soil through her patient, steady practice of mindfulness. She had watered the garden of her heart with the soft rain of her kind words and loving presence. And she had created the space for the young, tender shoot to grow in the light of her caring awareness. And this, she realized, would need nurturing to grow to its full potential, just like her own heart.

⟞ PRACTICE ⟝
Cultivating Self-Kindness

For this practice you will do a reflective meditation.

1. Find a place where you can be undisturbed for at least ten minutes. Sitting in a chair where you can be upright yet relaxed, assume a comfortable posture.

2. Gently close your eyes and turn your attention to your heart area, in the center of your chest. Feel your breath coming and going there. If it helps, place your hand on your chest as a way to connect more with your heart.

3. Take a few moments to connect with your inherent goodness. We all came into this world open, vulnerable, and with loving hearts. These beautiful qualities often get obscured as we grow up. Right now try to sense that innate goodness. If you find this difficult, then reflect on one positive quality you possess or one kind, skillful action you do that allows you to feel a positive regard for yourself. Or just connect to your basic wish to be happy.

4. Then offer these words to yourself slowly and meaningfully. Say one phrase silently with each out breath, and let the sentiment of the phrase reverberate through your body like ripples on the surface of a pond.

    "May I be safe and protected from harm."
    "May I be healthy."
    "May I be happy."
    "May I live with freedom and ease."
    "May I love and accept myself just as I am."

Say these phrases to yourself over and over, as genuinely as you can. If your critic tries to chastise you, simply ignore its words and keep repeating the phrases, gathering as much energy and intention as you can for each phrase. If it feels like the words are hitting a brick wall of numbness, try to imagine someone who loves you or who has been kind to you in the past offering those same words to you.

5. Now, as a gesture of love, call to mind people you know, and offer them these same words of kindness, changing the "I" in these phrases to "you."

6. When you feel ready to end this meditation, slowly open your eyes, and gently move and stretch.

As you go about your day, try to say these phrases to yourself. It is especially helpful to say them to yourself after each time the critic judges you. When responding to the critic, at the end of each judgment, you can add "and may I be happy" or "and may I love and accept myself just as I am."

As with any practice, if this is a new orientation for you, it can take time to become able to genuinely offer yourself these words of kindness. The more you practice, the more the qualities expressed in the loving phrases will become available to you.

CHAPTER TWENTY-SIX

TRANSFORMING PAIN

◄ ►

Moving from Self-Harm to Self-Compassion

If you want others to be happy, practice compassion. If you want to be happy, practice compassion.

— DALAI LAMA

James grew up in Somerset, England, in a strict Catholic family. He was sent to boarding school at age eleven. Mostly, he enjoyed the experience, except for one shadowy aspect that still haunts him today. As an altar boy, he had special duties to perform for the mass on Sunday, including arriving early to prepare the various ritual objects for the service.

His parents were proud he was serving in this way. It was, however, a very different experience for him. From the outset the priest had taken advantage of James and had forced him into sexual activity. He would come to dread those early morning times yet did not feel he could turn to anyone.

In time, as often happens, he blamed himself for the abuse. He doubted his innocence and wondered where he may have been at

fault. He lived with a sense of shame, compounded by his isolation and the fear that others would find out. This made it difficult
for him to have normal adolescent relationships, and in adulthood
those memories haunted him and scarred his sex life.

When he came to an intensive silent retreat, removed from
all his usual busyness at work and habitual online distractions, he
began to feel the shame from the past. The shame loomed large,
as if he were reliving some of those painful memories. His critic,
ever by his side, reminded him that it *was* his fault and that he
should feel guilty, that he only had himself to blame.

Sadly, I often encounter this kind of situation, where vic-
tims of childhood abuse blame themselves. When a parent is the
abuser, it is even harder for young children to imagine their parent would harm them. It is difficult for a young psyche to believe
their caregiver would exploit them. So they lay the blame at their
own feet. Having to undergo the original violation was horrific
enough. To then have to relive it and believe you were at fault,
and live with that shame, is a double tragedy.

In meditation, particularly on the retreats I lead, there is an
atmosphere of safety where everything is welcome. People are
given permission to allow whatever wants to happen in their inner
experience. The space created by slowing down, and having no
distractions of technology or conversation, allows for things to
rise up from deep in the psyche. Sometimes long-repressed memories can come up.

For James it was a radical thing to not only have time to be
with himself, but also, perhaps for the first time in his life, be in
a safe enough space to feel the turbulent emotions in his heart.
When he came in for an individual meeting, he shared a little
about his painful memories from childhood as an altar boy. But
very quickly he talked about how it was his fault and that he was
to blame. If only he were different, it would not have happened.

In our session I asked him if he would be willing to put aside those harsh views (from his critic) and simply feel how it was for that young boy to be abused in that way. To put himself in that boy's shoes and to allow the feelings that may be there. He said he would give it a try.

When he came back the next day, he said he'd been able, for the first time, to ignore the critical voices and instead feel the emotions beneath the critic's words. He felt his hurt, his anger, and his grief. When he ignored the judgmental voices, he was able to feel not just the pain, but also a sense of care or love toward that young boy. As he spoke, there were tears in his eyes. His whole demeanor seemed softer, his body more relaxed, and the lines of tension on his face had eased. He had been able to see that young boy through the eyes of an adult, with compassion.

This perspective changes everything. It takes us out of blame and into mercy. Compassion is the heart's healing balm and has the power to alleviate and transform suffering. It can resolve the pain that causes the critic to arise in the first place. From the perspective of the heart, harsh self-judgment and self-critical attacks like the ones James experienced are a form of cruelty. Compassion is a direct antidote to that and is ultimately what heals the cycle of pain and judgment.

Compassion has been described as a quivering of the heart in response to pain. It is intimate with the pain and distress of another or ourselves. In James's case he had to open viscerally to the sadness and hurt about being violated at such a young age in order for self-compassion to arise.

Mindfulness enables us to feel our pain, and compassion is the heart's response to that pain. Compassion wishes to help and to heal the suffering. Kindness and awareness, like the two wings of a bird, work together to release the force of compassion, which is essential to our work with the critic.

Many of the things we have self-judgments about are them-selves painful. For instance, a student I know is harsh with himself for being cognitively slower following a brain injury. A client, Sandra, berates herself for being overweight even though that is due mostly to developing diabetes. Sometimes we just feel over-whelmed by our parenting responsibilities or are fearful of some-thing, such as flying, and the judge lashes out at our supposed weakness.

All of these things are already painful enough. We don't need to add to our distress by listening to the critic. When instead we feel compassion for ourselves for having to endure these inner struggles, we are no longer at war with ourselves. We become our own ally, rather than our enemy in dealing with life's challenges.

This does require us to have the courage to probe the painful areas within and to not heed the critic's words. We can keep the critic at bay with a firm, compassionate stance just as we would take toward anyone who was hurting a friend who was already in pain. Compassion, unlike common assumptions about the quali-ties of the heart, is a courageous force that is fierce yet kind and attuned. Compassion does not flee from pain, or try to judge or get rid of it. It is simply there with a strong, kind presence. When we have access to this heartfulness, the critic loses much of its influence over us.

➤ PRACTICE ➤
Developing Self-Compassion

Turning toward our pain with compassion, rather than judg-ment or rejection, is a milestone when it comes to finding wholeness in our life. It is like bringing a calming salve to our aching emotional wounds and hurts. When we can ac-cess this attitude of self-care in times of distress and angst, it can shift the experience of pain from being unbearable to being tolerable and workable.

This meditation will help you learn to address your pain with compassion.

1. Find a place where you can be undisturbed for at least ten minutes. Sitting in a chair where you can be upright yet relaxed, assume a comfortable posture.

2. Gently close your eyes and feel your breath in your heart center, in the middle of your chest.

3. Call to mind any way that you are currently in pain, stressed, or suffering. It may be physical, emotional, mental, or spiritual pain. Or it could be difficult, stressful life circumstances or relationship woes.

4. Take some time to feel into the particular challenges and suffering involved in these experiences. Try to be with the pain, with a kind, caring attention. If judgments or other thoughts arise, acknowledge them and let them go.

5. While holding the pain with this kind, caring presence, say these phrases slowly and meaningfully to yourself, as if you were consoling a dear friend who was in distress:

    "May I be free of pain and suffering."

    "May I hold my suffering with kindness and ease."

6. If this practice accentuates the pain too much, then let go of focusing on the pain and take some slower, deeper breaths, and open your eyes until you feel centered again and not so lost in the pain.

Then resume saying the phrases and turning kindly toward your suffering.

7. Do this for five to ten minutes. Then, if it feels appropriate, you can extend compassionate wishes to other people you know who are in distress. Call them to mind, visualize them, feel into their pain, and offer them the phrases you used for yourself or some other compassionate phrases of your choosing.

8. When you feel ready to end this meditation, slowly open your eyes, and gently move and stretch.

After practicing this meditation a few times, you can offer these phrases to yourself at any time, whenever you are feeling pain or distress. You can also offer them to others whenever you encounter suffering.

CHAPTER TWENTY-SEVEN

GIVING UP HOPE OF A BETTER PAST

➤ ➤

From Self-Blame to Self-Forgiveness

It behooves every man to remember that the work of the critic is of alto-gether secondary importance, and that, in the end, progress is accomplished by the man who does things.

— THEODORE ROOSEVELT

When I ask a room full of students, "Who hasn't caused some-one harm through their words and actions?," not a single hand is ever raised. We have all done things we regret. I similarly ask if there is anyone who has not caused harm in some way through their sexuality. Again, rarely does a hand go up. It is the same when I ask if there is anyone who doesn't regret acting or saying something foolish in a moment of passion and reactivity.

Making mistakes, having poor judgment, and doing things we know we shouldn't in the heat of the moment are a natural part of the human condition. Why then are we so hard on ourselves? How do we account for all the self-blame? We can trace this pathology of self-recrimination to the critic and to an idealized and impossible standard of human behavior.

One of the things I've most appreciated about my years of meditation practice is having made peace with my humanness. It's not that I don't aspire to grow and develop and work on myself. But I'm no longer holding myself to some impossible ideal. The less I expect myself to be perfect and never mess up, the more likely I am to make headway toward forgiving myself. I am more able to release the heavy guilty burden I've been carrying for painful things I've done in the past, for the things I regret.

Sometimes I look back and am embarrassed at what I used to say, the views I espoused, and the self-centered hubris of youth. But that too is part of living, of growing up, the inevitable growing pains of being human. When I first discovered meditation, I was like a "born-again meditator," and I would enthusiastically try to convince all my friends and family that they should meditate. I was, in my youthful arrogance, eager to point out all the ways they were not enlightened and what they should do about it. Now my family teases me about that.

One particular realization I owe to my meditation training is an understanding that there is no time but now. The future is an illusion, the past is now a dream, and the only reality we have access to *is* the present. In that light, self-forgiveness is the willingness to stop trying to fix our past or make it better. It is giving up all hope of improving that which has already happened. What is done is done.

If this is true, then why do we try so hard to fix the past? It is because we can't bear to live with the painful fact that we did and said all those things that we regret and wish we could take back. We do it as a way to try and stop the pain that still lingers in the present from past events. The mind has a deep-seated resistance to feeling pain, even if it happened a long time ago. That is why we spend so much time in our head, thinking, replaying, rehashing, arguing, rather than acknowledging the tender, vulnerable part of ourselves and letting in the sadness and loss that accompanied the pain when it occurred.

I went to school in a rough part of town. There were constant physical fights, and harsh bullying was rife. Like so much human pain, it got passed down the chain, from the older kids to the younger kids. I was on the receiving end of a lot of painful bullying and psychological taunting. However, I also learned to dole it out. I would pass on the psychological ridicule I had received to others, when there was no risk of being physically threatened while doing so.

I used to look back with horror and shame on the ways that I teased and taunted a classmate. How could I, who knew how painful it was to be ridiculed in public, serve out the same? Given the space of time and some wise reflection, I can now see I was just a cog in the wheel, just passing on what I had learned, trying to survive in my own way and to keep the bullying attention away from myself. Find a scapegoat and stay safe was the motto. Of course, that does not in any way justify it or make it right. I still wonder to this day about the impact that my words and actions had on my poor classmate, and I still feel sad that I chose to act that way.

And it is self-forgiveness that allows me to understand the conditions of that period of my life and feel the pain of all involved; at the same time it allows me to release the judgment and shame. Even though I was the one being cruel, deep in my heart I also knew that it was mean and was fueled by my own pain and fear. It was what it was. It happened due to a painful set of causes and conditions, and I can feel tender toward myself, the classmate, and all the ways such actions continue today out of blindness, fear, and hatred.

In what ways do you judge yourself for your past errors? In what areas of life are you trying to make your past into a better one? In what ways are you unable to accept who and what you were? This is not about denying what happened or making it all better. It is about turning the light directly on the areas of painful regret and extending a loving hand to them.

Anytime we have an unusually large amount of space and time on our hands, our mind will ruminate on the paths of yore. This is partly the brain rehashing past experience in an attempt to learn for the future. In such times things from the dim and distant past that are still not resolved will surface in our hearts. This is especially true for those who have had brushes with death, are very sick, or are facing terminal illness. Given that we are social creatures, at these times our hearts may do a life review, with a particular focus on how we have acted in relation to others. This may certainly be about our romantic history, but it also includes our relationships with family, friends, colleagues, and neighbors.

I noticed this tendency in my father as he got older. He would occasionally ask about how he was as a father when I was young. In particular, he would inquire as to whether he was around enough or was gone too much. He served in the British Royal Navy, so he was absent for long stretches of time when I was an infant. I could tell it weighed heavily on his heart. There was nothing he could do about it now, yet something in his heart needed comforting and reassuring. And as much as I could offer assurance, it has to, as always, ultimately come from forgiving ourselves.

Any consideration of our relationships will inevitably reveal both joys and challenges. And, of course, it is easy fodder for the critic, who will pick on all the ways we have let people down, spoken falsely, hurt our loved ones, or just not shown up as a friend in ways we might have wished. These are often tender and painful memories to harbor. It is important that we hold these memories with compassion and kindness, not recrimination. It is all too easy for the judge with 20/20 hindsight to see all the ways we could have done better. But, as we explored in chapter 11, it's important to remember we always do the best we can with the information, skills, and resources we have available at the time.

So, as part of healing the heart and the past that keeps cascading into the present, we practice extending forgiveness to ourselves for our past choices and actions. We aim to fully accept what happened, take responsibility for it, and form a strong intention to learn from our past and live more wisely, with more care and compassion. We also extend forgiveness to ourselves in the present and for the future, knowing that, being human, we will make other choices that we may live to regret. We aspire to hold true to our intention to act with as much integrity and kindness as we can muster, but we forgive ourselves when we inevitably mess up.

In this way your practice of forgiveness becomes a positive mental habit, that allows you to release judgment, regret and the torment of shame from the past and present. And that opens the capacity for the loving heart to grow in all directions.

—— **PRACTICE** ——

Fostering Self-Forgiveness

Turning toward our mistakes with forgiveness rather than judgment or blame contributes significantly toward feeling peace in our heart. It is like bringing a soothing balm to painful parts of ourselves that we have long rejected. When we can access this attitude of forgiveness in times of distress and angst about something we have said or done, it can allow us to release that experience and be at greater ease.

This meditation will aid you in developing a sense of self-forgiveness.

1. Find a place where you can be undisturbed for at least ten minutes. Sitting in a chair where you can be upright yet relaxed, assume a comfortable posture.

2. Gently close your eyes and feel your breath in your heart center, in the center of your chest.

3. Call to mind one particular way that you have harmed others through your words or actions. It may be mental, emotional, or relational pain that was caused.

4. Take a few moments to feel into the experience and suffering of those involved in these memories. Can you be with their pain and angst with a kind attention?

5. Hold that pain with caring attention, and offer these words slowly and meaningfully to yourself:

No matter what I have done, knowingly or unknowingly, that has caused pain and suffering to others, by my thoughts, words, or actions, by what I have said or not said, by what I have done or not done, or by what I have thought, I offer myself forgiveness as much as is possible in this moment.

Repeat these phrases a few times while remembering what happened. Try to stay connected to your heart and allow all your feelings to be present. If the critic arises and reminds you how bad you are and why you should feel shame, shift your attention away from the judgment. Thank it for its opinion, then shift your attention back to the meditation and the phrases of forgiveness.

6. Now call to mind one particular way that you have harmed yourself. It may be physical or emotional harm, caused by self-neglect or by the way you punish yourself, mistreat your body, or disparage yourself in public.

7. Hold the pain of that incident with caring attention, and offer these phrases slowly and meaningfully to yourself:

No matter what I have done, knowingly or unknowingly, that has caused pain and suffering to myself, by my thoughts, words, or actions, by what I have said or not said, by what I have done or not done, or by what I have thought, I offer forgiveness to myself as much as is possible in this moment.

Stay present to whatever feelings, reactions, or pain comes up. Try to bring as much loving presence to yourself, to the feelings, and to the pain as possible. Say these phrases several times, slowly and genuinely, so you can let in whatever feelings may be present.

8. When you feel ready to end this meditation, slowly open your eyes, and gently move and stretch.

Know that when it comes to forgiving yourself, you may not, at first, feel much mercy at all. The key phrase in this practice is "as much as is possible in this moment." We do the best we can to begin the slow, patient path of forgiveness. Learning to forgive takes time, sometimes years. So be patient as you weave a little forgiveness into your daily routine as a way of strengthening your capacity to forgive.

It is also important to remember that we do not do this forgiveness exercise to gloss over any harmful wrongdoing, past or present. We practice forgiveness while also taking full responsibility for what we did. And then we aspire to not repeat such behavior in the future.

Once you learn to do this in formal meditation, you can bring the phrases of forgiveness to mind wherever you are.

PART FIVE

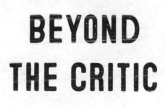

BEYOND
THE CRITIC

CHAPTER TWENTY-EIGHT

INCLINING TOWARD HAPPINESS

Paying Attention to the Good

Judgments prevent us from seeing the good that lies beyond appearances.

— WAYNE DYER

One of my favorite quotes about the mind is "Whatever the mind frequently dwells and ponders upon, that becomes the inclination of the mind." This applies equally to the heart. The meaning is that we are the product of what we do, think, and say. What we practice, we become. The lens we look through becomes our perspective. What our thoughts fixate upon becomes our reality.

The good news is you always have a choice in this. You have the power in every moment to shift toward habits of mind and heart that are healthy or harmful. The choice is yours. Which path do you want to take? What kind of world do you want to live in?

There is an ancient story of an old, wise gatekeeper who stood watch at the entrance to a walled city to interview new arrivals. Each person arriving for the first time would be asked where they were coming from, what kind of place they left, and what the people were like. To those who answered they were coming from a place where the people were mean, unfriendly, cold, and untrustworthy, he would say it was likely they would find the same here. To those who replied the people from the town they just left were warm, hospitable, friendly, and kind, he would again respond that it was likely they would find the same here. Same place, different reality. Which one would you choose?

Have you noticed that optimistic people generally tend to experience people and life in a brighter, more positive way? In contrast, those who focus on the negative, the problems, foibles, and flaws of others, tend to keep finding that life and the people in it are also flawed and problematic. Similarly, those who tend to look from the critic's vantage point tend to experience the world as a more negative place and the people in it as more difficult and troublesome.

I was once leading a seminar on the inner critic, at Esalen in Big Sur, California. Esalen is an exquisitely beautiful center perched on the cliffs facing the Pacific Ocean. It is as charming a place as you will find anywhere. As I was setting up the room for the seminar, the participants began to arrive. Slowly, one by one, they entered the room.

As each person came in, they all had something negative to say about the room. First the sitting cushions were too big. Then someone commented on the harsh lighting. Then a comment about the hardness of the chairs. Then a disparaging remark about the color of the carpet. Then a judgment about how I had advertised the class. After the fifth or sixth judgment, I asked myself what was going on. Then I realized that of course they were judgmental — it was a seminar on the inner critic, so guess who was bringing their critic to class. I then related to the class what I'd observed, and we could all see the humor in the situation: What do a bunch of critics do when they gather? They judge!

As discussed in chapter 6, this negativity bias comes from our evolutionary heritage. By focusing on what is wrong, what is dangerous and problematic, we learned to survive and navigate challenging circumstances. It was our nervous, critical, suspicious forebears who won the evolutionary battle, and that is what we inherit today.

However, our present circumstances are very different from the jungle or savannah. We no longer need a fight-or-flight hypervigilance against every threat we perceive. We don't need to view every person we meet as a potential foe. And we have to ask ourselves whether we want to view life from this negatively oriented perspective. Because if we do, we will surely feel and live in a world that we believe is more negative and riddled with fear, distrust, and suspicion.

Instead we can work to intervene when this hardwiring triggers a negatively slanted, critical orientation. As you read these words, notice if a strong argument is forming in your mind that it is not okay to trust, that it is good to always have your guard up, and that people, especially strangers, are not to be trusted. The critic may insist these things are true, but we don't have to listen to it.

The more we think and believe the ideas the critic puts forth, the more we strengthen the corresponding neural pathways, and the more entrenched that state of mind becomes. The more firmly we believe that life is faulty, just not good enough, the more likely we are to experience it that way. Fortunately, there is another way to live. We can begin to both notice our critic's negative bias and turn our attention to something more positive, and stop always seeing the glass as half-empty or insufficient.

I first began to do this when I lived in a residential retreat community. We would have periodic meetings where we gave each other constructive feedback, mostly leaning toward the positive but also pointing out each other's potential growth areas. We were encouraged to write down the positive stuff. This was useful because most people would immediately forget anything good that was said about them, since it didn't mesh with their self-image, and instead only focus on what was pointed out about themselves that needed some work.

After repeated exposure to this external reflection, I began to have a more objective view of myself. Instead of the long, dreary list of all my foibles and deficiencies, which my critic was keen to point out, I began to let in positive things about myself. As time went on, rather than dismiss the good things people had to say, if enough people said them, I began to believe that their shared perspective was more accurate than my own distorted one. I began to see myself in a different light. I developed a more balanced view that enabled me to see my strengths and gifts *and* the areas where I still needed to grow.

What would it be like to do that for yourself? To begin to see not just from the critic's vantage point, but also from one that allowed you to see the good, wholesome qualities you have? To see the thoughtful things you do and the kind words you say? At least the ones you do from time to time! You don't have to be an angel — just begin to see the ordinary good, human things you do and say.

Perhaps equally radical would be to begin to look at others that way. To not immediately see just their issues, neuroses, and problems. But instead to see the ways that people are also attentive, kind, helpful, generous, or industrious. Keep in mind that what you may label as "uptight" may just be someone who is organized, or what you might judge to be "lazy" may actually be someone who is relaxed and content.

You can also begin to take in the good in everything around you. What would it be like to pay more attention to the beauty of nature? Or to be thankful for the joy of friendship, love, or the company of an animal? Or to take in the things that are going well in your life or the blessings you already have, like access to clean water, safety, clothing, warmth, and food? Or to simply register that you have the time and education to be able to read this book? See what happens in your nervous system when you take in the goodness around you.

Savoring this, really taking this in, can slowly help nudge your heart in a much more uplifting and wholesome direction. But it is also important to remember this is a practice. It requires mindful attention to continuously notice the habit and direction of your mind and perception. What is key is to remember you have the power to change a particular negative habit in any moment, solely by changing what you choose to pay attention to.

━ PRACTICE ━

Reassessing Your Self-Perception

In your journal keep an ongoing list of your positive attributes — things about yourself that you or others notice or get reflected back to you by others.

Notice behaviors, actions, and ways you talk to or care for others that reflect positive qualities like generosity, kindness, and thoughtfulness. Stay open to feedback from others about the strengths and good qualities they notice and appreciate in you. Practice letting in their feedback. Notice any ways that you try to deflect, ignore, or write off any positive views about you or how you function in the world.

Similarly, at work, when you receive a performance review, practice taking in all the positive things that are noted and reflected back to you. Of course, you will also likely receive some constructive criticism; that is part of the process of a review. Your task, however, is to practice taking in the positive and appreciative words as a way to counterbalance the brain's negative orientation.

When you start orienting toward what is whole, good, and positive in yourself moment to moment, you will gradually shift your negative bias and begin to have a much more well-rounded and balanced view of yourself — both your strengths and your challenges.

CHAPTER TWENTY-NINE

WHO ARE YOU?

—◁ ▷—

Seeing the Good in Others

Love is the absence of judgment.

— DALAI LAMA

Rick Hanson gives a lovely example of how seeing the good in others, and sharing it with them, can have far-reaching consequences:

> Going through school, I was very young and therefore routinely picked last for teams in PE: not good for a guy's self-esteem. Then, my first year at UCLA, I gave intra-mural touch football a try. We had a great quarterback who was too small for college football. After one practice, he told me in passing, "You're good and I'm going to throw to you." I was floored. But this was the beginning of me realizing that I was actually quite a good athlete. His recognition also made me play better, which helped

our team. Thirty-five years later I can still remember his comment. He had no idea of its impact, yet it was a major boost to my sense of worth. In the same way, unseen ripples spread far and wide when we see abilities in others — especially if we acknowledge them openly.

We tend to think that our memory and our perception of ourselves — and others — is absolute fact. However, that notion has been seriously questioned by psychologists. Memory recall was considered a credible source in the past but has for some time come under attack. Forensics can now support psychologists in their claim that memories and individual perceptions are unreliable, being easily manipulated, altered, and biased. We need only call to mind our own memory of events to see how perception can get distorted and skewed.

Identification of subjects or their accounts of what happened in a crime scene are not always reliable since the data from such "evidence" is often contradictory. Sadly, people have been falsely accused and sentenced based on the testimony of witnesses who believed that what they perceived or remembered was fact.

In the same way, how often do we see people as they really are? Do we simply see them through the filter of our own biases, prejudices, and conditioned viewpoints? When the critic has been interfering with the hardware in our brain for a few decades, there is a high probability that what we see is distorted by interference from our judgmental mind.

As explained in chapter 13, our mind is like a revolving door — what goes out goes in, and vice versa. If we fixate on our own faults and shortcomings, then we will no doubt do the same when we turn attention to those around us, whether family, friends, colleagues, or strangers. We will be even harsher in assessing our enemies or those we regard as "other."

Try noticing what you observe in people as you sit in a café or in a meeting at work or as you watch them going about their day. Pay particular attention to what you see in people who seem different from you. Do you see their strengths and unique gifts? Do you see them in a kind, appreciative light?

Most likely, your mind gravitates toward things you feel critical about. The odd way they dress, the funny way they walk, or perhaps some physical or psychological trait that seems strange or problematic. It is also useful to register how what you notice about them makes you feel. Our mental and emotional state is affected by what we focus on. When we fixate on the negative or deficient in ourselves or others, it tends to make us feel contracted, separate, perhaps a little mean. Even when we focus on the negative in others to try to make ourselves feel better by comparison, it is ultimately unsatisfying because there will always be someone, somewhere who can outdo us. It leaves us in a state of perpetual agitation and fear.

What is the alternative? Writing this, I began to think of the parable of the Good Samaritan. It is a story that Jesus of Nazareth tells. When we see another as separate from us — even if they are in desperate need, as the traveler who is sick on a lonely road in the story is — we tend to focus on what is different from us, what we perceive to be wrong with them, and how they may be a threat. This leads us to close our heart and ignore or neglect them, especially in times of need. We see this kind of reaction all the time toward the homeless or new immigrants. Is this a state we want to live in, where our heart is closed in fear or coldness?

In the Good Samaritan story a traveler does overcome that initial barrier of difference and helps the sick person to safety even though the ailing man is from a different tribe. The traveler was able to overcome what was presumably his initial bias and see the truth that all people want to be safe and happy. He was able to access empathy for the sick person's plight, see that the person was just like him, and understand how easily the roles could be reversed in different circumstances.

Cutting through the bias of the negative, critical mind can help us see people in a different, fresh way. We can notice what unites us, not what divides us. We can sense our common humanity. We can also start to see the positive, bright, and uplifting characteristics of people who affect our own mind and heart in a positive way.

Just as focusing on the negative makes us feel negative and closed, so shifting our attention to people's positive qualities and strengths can brighten our mood and day. I know when I do this, it shifts me from feeling isolated to feeling warm and connected. I like to practice this when a person walks through the door of the room I am in. Instead of feeling an initial sense of caution or apprehension about who is entering the room, I instead focus on anything positive I can find, whether in the way they dress, their face, their smile, or anything I might know about them that I like.

Sometimes I will notice the impact of the practice of seeing the good in others when I'm around a friend who naturally does that all the time. When I'm with my friend Alice and we are talking about someone, no matter what the person has said or done, she can always find ways to see the positive, to focus on the goodness in that person. When she does that, I find my own sense of that person changing and my own inner state shifting toward something brighter and lighter.

─── **PRACTICE** ───

"Just Like Me" Meditation

This exercise helps cut through the usual barriers that make us feel separate or different from others. It is a way we can actively sense our connection with other people, partly by focusing on our shared human experiences. Next time you are talking with someone, in a meeting at work, looking at others in a café or on the street, or at your children's school with other parents, reflect on these phrases:

- Just like me, this person wants to be happy.
- Just like me, this person wishes to be free of pain and stress.
- Just like me, this person has a body subject to aches, pains, and aging.
- Just like me, this person has had many joys and successes.
- Just like me, this person has felt sadness, loss, and pain.
- Just like me, this person desires to love and be loved.
- Just like me, this person aspires to do their best in life.
- Just like me, this person wants peace and happiness.

As you do this, notice how it makes you feel. Does it allow for any sense of feeling connected? Know that you can return to this sentiment in any moment and see how it can transform your experience of someone as being other to seeing them as being just like you, with all of your shared human experiences.

Try to practice saying these phrases wherever you go. You can also do this exercise as a meditation where you sit quietly, call to mind particular people, and say the phrases to yourself.

Saying these phrases to yourself is particularly useful when you are having a conflict or a challenging time with someone. The more you can sense the similarities between you and them and see they are not other, the more likely you will be to feel a sense of connection and find it easier to relate to them.

CHAPTER THIRTY

INNER PEACE

━ ▬ ▬

A Life beyond the Critic

Whatever I do is done out of sheer joy; I drop my fruits like a ripe tree.
What the general reader or the critic makes of them is not my concern.

— HENRY MILLER

What would life be like if you were no longer persecuted by the critical voices in your head and lived your life as Henry Miller describes — doing things out of sheer joy, unconcerned about the critic? Imagine you had been walking around with a sixty-pound backpack and suddenly put that weight down. How would that feel? Like an incredible relief, a great lightening of the load! This is how it can feel to live free from the critic.

The title of Milan Kundera's novel *The Unbearable Lightness of Being* has always struck me as a great expression for what happens when the burden of self-judgment is lifted. Life without the critic does have a lightness to it. It has a sense of ease, playfulness, and inner peace.

When I encounter people who are freed from the millstone of

the critic, it is as if they have a "get out of jail free" card in the Monopoly game. They get to play an easier hand in life than others. They are not caught up in self-recrimination, second-guessing, and fixating on their problems or faults. They view mistakes as learning opportunities, can laugh at their foibles, and smile when they can't find their keys.

They seem to be optimists, viewing others with appreciative eyes. They recover easily from setbacks. They look at the world with the attitude that the glass is half-full; the glass half-empty is simply not an option.

We may have experienced times in our life when we felt this way. Or perhaps through applying the techniques described in this book, we feel some distance from the impact of our critic. At these moments, we get a taste of inner quiet, where our mind is no longer looking for what is wrong or how we failed. Instead it has a more balanced perspective that allows us to see our gifts and strengths and accurately assess our challenges.

Perhaps most importantly, we learn that regardless of whether the tirade of self-judgment stops, we can find space and ease, and no longer identify with our condemning thoughts. We can understand that we no longer need to listen to or believe the critical voices. We can simply experience them like the sound of birds chattering in the trees, which don't affect us. It is as if our heart had suddenly been coated with Teflon and whatever insults come from the inner tyrant simply wash off like rainwater.

Another significant outcome from learning how to meet and defuse the harsh self-judgment is a shift in our self-worth. Years of tireless put-downs from the judge take their toll. They can leave us feeling depressed, hopeless, and worthless. They can rob us of a sense of our basic goodness.

However, as we begin to see ourselves not through the lens of the critic, but through the lens of a kind, clear, and wise attention, we start to sense our innate goodness. We learn we are not all bad and that we have many gifts, qualities, and strengths. We discover that it *is* our birthright to take our place in the world, regardless of what we have done, said, or accomplished. We can access a sense of well-being and contentment that allows us to love and appreciate ourselves just as we are.

This is a far cry from being in the grip of an inner critic that is always berating us because we don't do more, do better, or aim higher. Instead we find ourselves at ease in our own skin and not on a relentless path of self-improvement to appease the critic. So we are more likely to find inner contentment and genuine self-love.

Another sign of being at peace with the judging mind is when we can relate to the critic wisely and understand that whenever the arrows are thrown, there is usually some trigger — an underlying cause, hurt, or need that can be inquired into and understood. We learn how to turn to ourselves with a kind heart in that moment of vulnerability or anxiety rather than persecuting ourselves.

The more we bring awareness and love to our internal struggles, the less room there is for judgments to erode our sense of self-worth, and the more we feel integrated, whole, and at peace with ourselves.

We all have the ability to diminish the critic's attacks, quiet its voice, and soften the impact of its judgments. I have worked with many students worldwide who have been able to find significant relief from understanding, defending, and freeing themselves from the torment of self-hatred and self-judgment.

And in the meantime, until that freedom is realized, you can still put some distance between yourself and the judgments in any moment by applying one of the remedies discussed in this book. We can say "No" to the critic, thank it for its opinion, or just observe its judgments in the light of mindful awareness. We can remember that the judgment is just a thought, a point of view, not ultimate truth or something we need to listen to or believe. Or we can simply sense the vulnerability and fear from which the critical words come and turn to ourselves with kindness and forgiveness.

In any moment, you can set aside the burden of the critic's judgments and taste freedom, using the tools of mindfulness, wisdom, and compassion.

━ PRACTICE ━

Noticing the Peace between Thoughts

All too often what grabs our attention in life is our thoughts. One Thai meditation expert's response to a question about how he would describe his students was that they were "lost in thought." We are addicted to our thinking and give it far too much attention, to the detriment of our other senses and the fullness of life going on around us. Total absorption in our thoughts also robs us of finding peace here and now.

Sometimes all we notice is our critical, judging thoughts. However, as much as that can be true, there is also plenty of time when the critic is not predominant and our mind is quiet. From a meditation *and* mental health perspective, it is very helpful to notice these moments of quiet, these gaps between our thoughts. If all we focus on is our thoughts and judgments, then that is all we will see. If instead we focus on the space after one thought ends and before another begins, we may find to our surprise that there is more quiet and stillness than we believed.

Use the following meditation to practice noticing the peaceful gaps between your thoughts.

1. Find a place where you can be undisturbed for at least ten minutes. Sitting in a chair where you

can be upright yet relaxed, assume a comfortable posture.

2. Gently close your eyes and take some time to sit quietly and focus on your breath. Or if you are in a place where there is a lot of noise, focus on the sounds. If you notice the pull of thoughts, judgments, or criticism try shifting your focus to your breath, to the sounds around you, or to other physical stimuli, and notice how the thoughts can recede.

3. See if you can observe quiet moments between judgments and other thoughts where there is simply physical, organic life happening by itself — sitting, breathing, listening, feeling, and watching.

4. Can you sense any quality of space, ease, or openness? Sense the peacefulness of these moments.

5. Feel into the simplicity and naturalness of being present.

6. Be open to the possibility that nothing else needs to happen, that everything in this moment is fine, perhaps whole and complete just as it is, including you.

7. When you feel ready to end this meditation, slowly open your eyes, and gently move and stretch.

This meditation is a simple way to access peace here and now. The more you practice noticing the space between your thoughts, and the more you rest in the awareness of the coming and going of thoughts, the more space you will begin to perceive in your inner experience. You will see that there are many opportunities to be quiet and still, and you will begin to find more of a natural ease in the present moment.

An alternative technique is to imagine your mind is a vast, clear, blue sky and the clouds are simply specks or puffs. Practice noticing and resting in all that spaciousness of awareness and not fixating on the clouds. This will help you gain a sense of the vastness and tranquillity of your true nature, a sense that is available to you anytime, anywhere.

CHAPTER THIRTY-ONE

THE CRITIC TOOLBOX

◄ ►

Defending Yourself against Judgments

To avoid criticism say nothing, do nothing, be nothing.

— ELBERT HUBBARD

A s you've probably realized, working with the critic does not just involve reading a book or going to a weekend workshop. To deal with a mental process that has been developing over most of your life requires much more than that. Over that time the inner critic has become intertwined with your thinking, your identity, your choices and actions.

To work with the critic effectively takes multiple strategies for countering those negative voices, entrenched views, and inaccurate ideas about who you are.

Every skilled craftsperson has a good toolkit for dealing with whatever issues arise in their trade. To hone the craft of our lives, we need equally fitting tools for dealing with the inner critic. What follows is a list of tried and tested strategies for defending yourself against the force of self-judgment. I call this set of strategies "the critic toolbox."

These tools have been described in preceding chapters and are presented here as some of the key components for an ongoing freedom from the judge. If you cultivate these tools, they will serve you for the rest of your life.

Mindfulness

Mindfulness, the capacity to be aware, to know ourselves, our thoughts, feelings, body, heart, and mind, is an indispensable tool. (Mindfulness is discussed in chapter 16.) Without that awareness, we can't even see the critical thoughts. Nor are we able to step back from the judgments and see them with any objectivity.

Mindfulness is not just something we need at the beginning, but a skill that we want to keep in our toolbox for a lifetime. No matter how effectively we deal with the judging mind, it always has the potential to rear its head when we are tired, overwhelmed, or have done or said things we regret. To be able to draw on this mindful awareness when we need it, we must practice and cultivate it on a daily basis. This can be done as described in a formal way, where we set aside time every day to cultivate a clear, focused attention to our inner experience. It can also be cultivated informally through consciously summoning our awareness when we are walking, talking, working, creating art or music, exercising, playing a sport — or doing anything.

However, what distinguishes developing this skill in meditation is that when we do so, we are focusing on our internal experience — mental, emotional, and physical — to understand ourselves more intimately. It is through turning this lens of attention inward over and over, with a sense of inquisitiveness, that we become familiar with our critical mind, its origins, and its physical and emotional impacts. The more we are alert to the critic's causes and effects, the more likely we are to be able to mitigate its impact on us.

Counting Your Judgments

To strengthen your capacity to recognize judgments, it can be helpful to count them. This initially helps you see how many there are. But it also alerts you to how incessant, nagging, and undermining they are. This strategy can help bring you some detachment. It can also elicit a sense of humor. After the fiftieth judgment about one small thing you did wrong, it makes it easier not to take the critic so seriously. And when you get to four or five hundred judgments in a day, the sheer volume of judgments makes them appear ridiculous.

Feeling the Impact of Judgments

Once you have observed your self-judgments, you need to feel the pain of being attacked by the judge. Normally, we are closely allied with our critic, so we stay aligned with it. However, when we shift our attention to our heart, to feel how it is to be spoken to so harshly, we open to the deep pain of it. It is as if our heart gets bruised by the critic's abusive words.

When we allow this to happen, we can more easily shift our perspective from the vantage point of the critic to that of the one who is being attacked, hurt, and belittled. Once we realize that the critic is causing us so much pain, it allows us to feel self-compassion. When our heart is engaged, it becomes a powerful force for standing up against further self-judgment.

Speaking to the Pain of Judgments

It can be helpful to speak to your critic (or yourself) about the pain you feel when you are on the receiving end of judgments.

This is something you might ordinarily do if a loved one spoke to you in a hurtful way. In response to a judgment from your critic, you might say, "Ow, that hurts," or "It's really painful when you talk to me like that." Even though it may sound like an odd thing to do with your critic, it shifts your allegiance from the judge to the part of you that is hurt by the judgments. It is a gentle but firm way of saying "No" and making it clear that such communication is ineffective and unacceptable.

The RAIN Exercise

RAIN is a practice that helps you work with painful emotions that arise from self-judgment. *RAIN* is an acronym for the process of *recognizing*, *allowing*, *inquiring*, and *not identifying* with feelings that arise. It helps you hold your emotions so you can explore them more fully and find greater ease.

The first step is *recognizing*. This is simply acknowledging an emotion when it is triggered by the critic. You can do this by labeling it to clarify what is actually present, such as by saying, "sadness" or "despair."

The next step is *allowing*, accepting the present emotions as they are. With this attitude you try to bring a welcoming acceptance to the emotion, to simply let it be there, without trying to judge or reject it.

The third step is *inquiring* into the emotional experience. This doesn't mean thinking or analyzing the emotion but simply bringing your attention closer to it to understand it with awareness, with an attitude of curiosity and interest. For example, try to sense how and where you experience the emotion physically. You can also pay attention to what triggered the emotion and what allows it to fade.

The last step is *not identifying* with the emotion or not taking it personally. With this perspective you can better understand how everything comes and goes according to causes and conditions. The emotion doesn't define who you are. It is simply a visitor.

Once you have explored a particular emotion, you can apply the RAIN process to any other feeling that is present. The point isn't to get rid of the emotions but to create greater acceptance and understanding of your emotional experience. You can learn to apply this technique throughout the day, wherever you are.

The Judgment Might Be True — So What!

One of the obstacles to not standing up for oneself to the critic is that we sometimes believe the judgments are true. Often the critic *is* pointing out something that is true. Maybe you did forget your best friend's birthday. Perhaps you forgot to reply to an email, or you were late picking the kids up from school. And because we know that is true, we can be apt to let the critic bash us with its judgment tirelessly, day after day. And the judging can go on years after the event that precipitated it has passed.

But the fact that something is true does not justify the critic's using it as ammunition to undermine our self-worth. It does not warrant the critic's haranguing us fifty times a day. The critic's rationale is that if it gets on your case enough, you will stop making mistakes, messing up, forgetting things, or causing yourself embarrassment and trouble. However, chastising anyone is rarely a good motivator for habit correction or action. It just makes you feel bad.

Would you let a friend walk around with you all day, telling you all the things you have done wrong that day and in the past? Probably not. You would just say, "Yes, you told me that once before, and I get it. I plan to address this or make amends. Now drop it or leave me alone. You don't need to remind me about it again and again."

You can employ a similar strategy with the critic. With a

simple acknowledgment you can say to the critic, "Yes, I heard it the first time. I got it, thanks. I don't need to hear this anymore."

Martial Arts Maneuver

This strategy is like a martial arts maneuver that flows with the energy movement of the judgments rather than trying to push back against it. Normally, in the face of a critic's assault, we try to push back against the attack. Perhaps we rationalize and justify all the ways we are good and the ways the critic is wrong. Instead of getting into that pointless argument, we can say, "Thank you for your point of view." And you can add, "I see you are trying to help, but no thanks."

Sometimes this takes the wind out of the critic's sails, in the same way that when a person is looking for a good argument and you agree with them, it can deflate their balloon. We are not looking for an argument with the critic. We are simply acknowledging it, yet not giving it the time of day. We let it pass through us, like wind through our hair.

What you are also acknowledging is that the critic's words are simply what they are — just a point of view, but not absolute truth. They are limited perceptions carved from a narrow viewpoint from the past. This perspective can help us experience them as less of a burden and prevent them from taking root in our heart.

Disinterest

Sometimes my first line of defense is disinterest. For example, when I'm driving to work and I realize I'm going to be late, that is a predictable cue for my critic to start ranting about how I should have left earlier, how I should be more efficient with time, and on and on. When that happens, usually my response is, "Oh, really," as in, "How predictable is that?" I might even say sarcastically, "Do you have anything else to say?" Since I have heard it all before, I am not that bothered by it. It is just background noise that I don't pay any attention to. It slides off me like water off a duck's back.

Humor

When we can see the humor or folly of all the critic's judgments, we become less identified with them, and they will stick less. When we playfully tease the critical voice, we don't take it so seriously anymore. A cousin of humor is sarcasm, which can also help us disengage from the judgments. For example, you could respond to a critical thought by saying, "Oh, that's really helpful. I wish I had thought of that!"

When I was on intensive meditation retreats and my critic was particularly vehement about dismissing my meditation attempts, I used humor to defuse its attacks. I would imagine my critic dressed up as on old English judge, with a long gray wig, saying in a very stern voice, "You are a bad meditator." Seeing it that way, I had to laugh at the silliness of giving this voice the right to rule over my experience.

Exaggeration

Exaggerating judgments is a useful antidote to the sting of the critic's voice. We expand the judgments to their utmost size and thereby see how crazy they are. You can also do this to rebut the critic's implication that you are worthless. For example, I might tell my critic, "Yes, I am the worst person to ever meditate. I am the most lousy teacher in the world. And now that you mention it, I'm the worst cook on earth too!" We take hold of the reins and embrace the judgments playfully. Of course, this only works if we don't actually believe the exaggerations! If you do, then you might not want to use this strategy.

Inquiry

The process of inquiry, which we utilize to question the validity of the critic's judgments (as discussed in chapter 21) is another invaluable tool on this journey. When turning the light of awareness toward our thoughts and judgments, we need a clarity of discernment to probe carefully and understand these often murky realms. In particular, we need to investigate the origins and causes of our harshest judgments so we can know how to dis-identify with them.

In addition, if we can bring a compassionate inquiry to our mental and psychological processes, it can enable us to both welcome and hold them with caring attention, rather than fight with them. This, in turn, facilitates the investigation that allows us to get to the root of why we can be so harshly critical and dismissive of ourselves and ultimately allows us to release the habit of doing so.

Is It True?

At times it is helpful to use a cognitive approach and question the truth of the judgments when they are inaccurate (which they mostly are). When we see they are not actually true, they tend to lose their bite. This strategy is especially appropriate when the judgments come with the words "always," "never," and "should." These words are a signal that the critic is at play. So when you hear, "You will never get your life together," "You are always late," or "You should be over your grief by now," you know the critic is present. It is easy to challenge the accuracy of these accusations. And when they involve anything in the future, we can be sure they are not true. Not one of us knows what will happen in the future, and "always" and "never" just don't apply to something that is yet to come.

Constructive Dialogue

To use this technique, imagine you are sitting down with someone you are in conflict with, someone who is reacting to you blindly, and simply ask: "What is going on? What are you trying to say? What is going on underneath these judgments and attacks? What do you need to resolve this? What are you afraid is going to happen?" With this kind of inquiry you are digging into the more subtle layers of fears and concerns that lie behind the critic's words. The critic's delivery may not be so helpful, but often it is pointing to valid concerns.

Who Do You Think You Are?

In addition to questioning its judgments, you can challenge the critic itself. You may ask it who it thinks it is to judge what you do. You might say in a strong manner, "Who are you to question my good intentions, my potential, or my innate value?" Sometimes finding your voice this way can help connect you with a sense of strength and personal power, something the critic may have eroded over time.

Firmness: Enough Is Enough

There are many times, especially when we first start working with the critic, when we need to stand up to it in a very direct way. At such times, we can meet the critic's attacks with the powerful energy of "No." Just as we might stand up to someone when a friend or child is being hurt, we can step in with a fierce protectiveness, like a mother bear.

We can say, "Enough is enough. Stop these attacks and back

off." Sometimes we have the power and energy to feel that "No," and we can confidently say, "Shut up, stop this, and go bother someone else." You may add your own expletives to enhance this emphatic statement! When we do that, we are defending ourselves in a protective way, not through anger or reaction, but out of an impulse born of a healthy love for ourselves and out of a wise sense of self-protection. The passion this can summon or release is part of a force the psyche needs at times, to defend itself against harmful attacks to our well-being.

Every strategy has its limits, which is why we need a large toolbox. And we have to be careful not to start an inner war. We are not making the critic an enemy. We are just saying "No" to its barbs in a forthright way. When we summon the inner strength to do so, we can create an inner space so we have room to feel, be with, and process what is going on within us. This gives us the space to be who we are. We can breathe.

Fierce Compassion

This strategy is based on a stance of fierce compassion. It is strong, grounded, heartfelt. It is the love that says, "Do not talk to me like that. It's too painful to bear, too harsh to feel the brunt of those words." Just as you might say to someone who was talking to you or a friend in a harsh or hurtful way. We stand up for ourselves with an open-hearted strength.

Replacing

This strategy replaces the judging thought with a neutral thought. When you replace the judgment with a neutral thought, the idea is to realize that the judgments are just a bunch of words. Learning to replace the critic's words with neutral statements like "The sky is blue" or "Grass is green" reminds you that the judgments are just words that only have the power you choose to give them.

Loving-Kindness

Loving-kindness is the capacity that enables us to shift from self-judgment to self-kindness (as discussed in chapter 25). It is by bringing love and kindness to ourselves instead of harshness and self-rejection that we can truly become an ally rather than an enemy of ourselves.

When we learn to be kind to ourselves, we become better equipped to deal with critical barbs when they come toward us from outside or within. Instead of siding with the harsh criticisms, we can find a kind inner support, as well as the clarity to discern which aspects of the judgments may be valid or useful and which are just attacks on our essential value that are better ignored or released.

To do this we must first connect with our basic goodness. We must remember that we have a right to exist, to be here, to claim our place on this earth. We must remember that we came into this world open, vulnerable, and loving and that we worked hard to fit in and be loved and accepted as we grew up. We all did what we needed to do to survive.

Secondly, we must begin to replace the harsh words of the critic with a kind, caring, and appreciative attitude toward ourselves. This can be done in a formal way through loving-kindness meditation. But even more importantly, it can also be done anywhere at any time by turning toward ourselves with warmth and repeating kind wishes for ourselves — phrases like "May I be well, healthy, happy, and at peace," "May I be free from pain and stress," or "May I love and accept myself just as I am."

Saying these phrases with sincerity, and allowing the words to settle into our body and heart, can have a profound healing effect over time. They help us turn toward ourselves with a caring and loving attitude. With their help, we can become our own best friend, one that never leaves our side, one that is there for us in times of distress and hardship.

Wisdom

The final tool, wisdom, arises out of all our work with the critic. This is the learning that comes from studying the causes and patterns of the judging mind, what triggers it, how we get caught up in it, and how we live our lives in fear of its wrath. (The origin and function of the critic are discussed in chapter 6.)

With wisdom we can see that the critic's viewpoint is skewed. We understand that it gets triggered when we mess up, are vulnerable, or get scared. And with discernment we can see that we don't have to listen to it, let alone believe it. At times, we can see there may be a grain of truth in what it is saying, but we don't take in the emotionally laden heaviness that is attached to or implied in its words. We no longer need to internalize the negative implications about our self-worth. As we develop this wisdom, we begin to see the critic more clearly, which can foster an amused, detached perspective, like that of a grandmother watching over her grandchildren, caring but unperturbed by their antics.

This wisdom also reminds us of the goodness of our nature, that we are okay as we are, even with all our human foibles and idiosyncrasies. It allows us to hold it all with a balanced equanimity. Wisdom enables us to rest in the truth that we are fine as we are *and* could all do with some work here and there. It helps us remember that our basic nature is good and complete just as it is. This knowledge allows us to come to peace, the very thing we so often search for, forgetting it was right here all along.

Further Reading

Brach, Tara. *Radical Acceptance: Embracing Your Life with a Heart of a Buddha*. New York: Bantam, 2004.

Brown, Byron. *Soul without Shame: A Guide to Liberating Yourself from the Judge Within*. Boston: Shambhala, 1998.

Carson, Rick. *Taming Your Gremlin: A Surprisingly Simple Method for Getting Out of Your Own Way*. Rev. ed. New York: Quill, 2003.

Neff, Kristin. *Self-Compassion: The Proven Power of Being Kind to Yourself*. New York: HarperCollins, 2015.

Stone, Hal, and Sidra Stone. *Embracing Your Inner Critic: Turning Self-Criticism into a Creative Asset*. San Francisco: HarperSanFrancisco, 1993.

ACKNOWLEDGMENTS

—◄ ►—

This work has come about through many years of study in different traditions. My first introduction to working with the inner critic came through the Diamond Approach of A. H. Almaas. I am forever indebted to his profound work of inquiry for teaching me how we can recognize and fiercely free ourselves from the oppression of the critic. I have also been influenced by Byron Brown, whose work *Soul without Shame*, on the inner critic from the perspective of the Diamond Approach, was groundbreaking.

I have much gratitude for my meditation teachers and colleagues in the Insight Meditation tradition, who have not only paved the way for the introduction of mindfulness teachings in the West but also allowed me to study those ancient practices. It is the gift of mindfulness that has enabled me to understand my own mind and to have insight and clarity about the workings of the inner critic. In particular, I wish to thank my primary teachers, Joseph Goldstein, Christopher Titmuss, and Jack Kornfield, whose pioneering work and kind guidance have been of immense help to me and countless others. I also offer a bow to all my teaching colleagues at Spirit Rock Meditation Center for their ongoing support and camaraderie over the years.

Love is indispensable for learning to work with the negative forces of the judging mind with compassionate care, without which healing would be impossible. In that light, I'm deeply grateful to Sharon Salzberg, whose teachings on loving-kindness and compassion have had a profound effect on my own practice and the hearts and minds of so many.

Similarly, I wish to appreciate Tara Brach for her teachings on radical (self-)acceptance and Kristin Neff for her pioneering research on the vital role of self-compassion. I also wish to acknowledge His Holiness the Dalai Lama, who is a beacon and role model of compassion and who categorically states that not liking oneself is not only a mistaken view but a profound misconception of who we really are.

Good friends on the path are essential, and I feel blessed to have friends who have helped illuminate my understanding of the critic as well as find humor in it, including Randall Alifano, Martin Aylward, Kelly Boys, Eugene Cash, Howie Cohn, Vince Draddy, Sharda Rogell, and Rick Smith. In that same vein, I wish to acknowledge one of my teachers, Sara Hurley, who has supported me in the journey of presence and whose good humor and guidance have been essential in my developing a loving relationship with myself. Similarly, I wish to thank so many friends too numerous to mention for all their kindness and support over the years.

I wish to honor my beloved Lori for all her steady support, patience, love, and unwavering confidence in me, especially during the writing of this book. I deeply appreciate the ways that she sees me and helps reflect the goodness of my own nature.

Appreciations to my publisher, New World Library, for all the work in producing this book, especially to Jason Gardner for his editorial support and faith in my work and to copyeditor Mark Colucci for his fine editing skill.

Finally, these acknowledgments would not be complete without mentioning how much I have learned from my students' struggles and insights with the judging mind over the past two decades. They have taught me to understand both the power of the critic and the ways that people are able to find a genuine transformation and release from its grip. I feel deep gratitude for their work and hard-earned victories. It is to them and the innumerable others afflicted by the critic that I dedicate this book.

NOTES

◀ ▶

Introduction: How I Discovered the Critic and Found a Way Out

Page 3   *Anne Lamott*: Anne Lamott, "My Mind Is a Bad Neighborhood I Try Not to Go into Alone," *Salon*, March 13, 1997, www.salon .com/1997/03/13/lamott970313/.

Chapter 2. You Are Not Alone: The Epidemic of Self-Judgment

Page 20   *One in ten Americans*: Laura A. Pratt, Debra J. Brody, and Qiuping Gu, "Antidepressant Use in Persons Aged 12 and Over: United States, 2005–2008," *NCHS Data Brief* 76 (October 2011), www.cdc.gov/nchs/data/databriefs/db76.pdf.

Page 20   *One in five took*: Brendan L. Smith, "Inappropriate Prescribing," *Monitor on Psychology* 43, no. 6 (2012), www.apa.org/monitor /2012/06/prescribing.aspx.

Page 20   *The number of suicides*: Gregg Zoroya, "40,000 Suicides Annually, yet America Simply Shrugs," *USA Today*, October 9, 2014, http://www.usatoday.com/story/news/nation/2014/10/09 /suicide-mental-health-prevention-research/15276353/.

Page 20   *Many industrialized countries*: Caroline Davies, "Number of Suicides in UK Increases, with Male Rate Highest since 2001," *Guardian*, February 19, 2015, www.theguardian.com/society/2015/feb/19 /number-of-suicides-uk-increases-2013-male-rate-highest-2001.

Chapter 3. Imposter Syndrome:
If They Really Knew Who I Am…

Page 23 *70 percent of people*: Jaruwan Sakulku and James Alexander, "The Imposter Phenomenon," *International Journal of Behavioral Science* 6, no. 1 (2011): 73–92.

Page 24 *Meryl Streep*: Kristin Shorten, "High-Achievers Suffering from 'Imposter Syndrome,'" December 10, 2013, www.news.com.au /finance/highachievers-suffering-from-imposter-syndrome /story-e6frfm1i-1226779707766.

Page 24 *Einstein admitted*: Caroline Ferguson, "Imposter Syndrome," accessed May 29, 2016, http://carolineferguson.com/imposter -syndrome/.

Page 24 *John Steinbeck*: John Steinbeck, *Working Days: The Journals of* The Grapes of Wrath, *1938–1942*, ed. Robert DeMott (New York: Penguin, 1990), entries 52, 56.

Page 24 *Sheryl Sandberg*: Olivia Goldhill, "Brilliant 'Frauds': Is Imposter Syndrome a Sign of Greatness?," *Quartz*, February 1, 2016, http://qz.com/606727/is-imposter-syndrome-a-sign-of-greatness/.

Chapter 5. You Are Not Your Fault:
Not Taking Your Thoughts Personally

Page 36 *Sixty to seventy thousand thoughts*: "Brain Trivia," Laboratory of Neuro Imaging, University of Southern California, accessed 6/8/2016, http://www.loni.usc.edu/about_loni/education /brain_trivia.php.

Chapter 6. How Did I Get Here?
The Origin and Function of the Critic

Page 42 *Sheryl Sandberg*: Sheryl Sandberg, *Lean In: Women, Work, and the Will to Succeed* (New York: Knopf, 2013), 19.

Chapter 10. The Mantra of "Not Enough":
Knowing When Enough Is Enough

Page 72 *philosopher Lao-tzu*: "Laozi," *Wikiquote* [citing *Tao Te Ching*, chap. 46], last modified April 23, 2016, https://en.wikiquote.org/wiki /Laozi.

Page 73 *Suicide rates went up:* Christopher Harress, "Suicide among Bankers Appears to Be on the Rise Again as Pressures to Get Banks and Businesses Back in the Black Takes Its Toll," *International Business Times,* September 4, 2013, www.ibtimes.com/suicide-among-bankers -appears-be-rise-again-pressures-get-banks-businesses-back-black -1402450.

Chapter 12. The Inner Boardroom: Understanding the Voices in Your Head

Page 88 *François Fénelon:* François Fénelon, *The Spiritual Letters of Archbishop Fénelon: Letters to Women,* trans. H. L. Sidney Lear (London: Longmans, Greene, 1900), 29.

Chapter 16. Mindfulness: The Power of Awareness

Page 111 *Nearly 330,000 injuries:* "Cell Phone Use While Driving Statistics," Edgar Snyder & Associates, accessed May 29, 2016, www.edgar snyder.com/car-accident/cause-of-accident/cell-phone/cell-phone -statistics.html.

Page 111 *National Safety Council:* Ibid.

Page 111 *multitasking on the job:* Travis Bradberry, "Multitasking Damages Your Brain and Career, New Studies Suggest," *Forbes,* October 8, 2014, www.forbes.com/sites/travisbradberry/2014/10/08 /multitasking-damages-your-brain-and-career-new-studies -suggest; Adam Gorlick, "Media Multitaskers Pay Mental Price, Stanford Study Shows," *Stanford News,* August 24, 2009, https://news.stanford.edu/2009/08/24/multitask-rsearch-study -082409/.

Page 111 *A large study:* Steve Bradt, "Wandering Mind Not a Happy Mind," *Harvard Gazette,* November 11, 2010, http://news.harvard.edu /gazette/story/2010/11/wandering-mind-not-a-happy-mind/.

Page 113 *In another study:* Timothy D. Wilson et al., "Just Think: The Challenges of the Disengaged Mind," *Science,* July 4, 2014.

Chapter 21. Reality Check: Are Your Judgments Really True?

Page 142 Byron, Katie, www.thework.com, The Four Questions.

Chapter 23: Befriending Yourself: You Are Not Your Enemy

Page 153 *Carl Jung*: Carl Gustav Jung, *Collected Works of C.G. Jung*, vol. 13, *Alchemical Studies*, ed. and trans. Gerhard Adler and R. F. C Hull. (New York: Princeton University Press, 1967), para 335, pages 265–266.

Page 158 *This being human is a guest house*: Jalāl al-Dīn Rūmī, "The Guest House," in *Essential Rumi*, trans. Coleman Barks. (San Francisco: HarperOne, 2004), 109.

Chapter 29: Who Are You? Seeing the Good in Others

Page 195 *Rick Hanson gives a lovely example*: Rick Hanson, "See the Good in Others," November 17, 2011, http://www.rickhanson.net/see-the-good-in-others/.

Chapter 30: Inner Peace: A Life beyond the Critic

Page 204 *Thai meditation expert's response*: Jack Kornfield, *After the Ecstasy, the Laundry: How the Heart Grows Wise on the Spiritual Path* (New York: Bantam, 2000), 35.

INDEX

◄— ►

ABOUT THE AUTHOR

= ▶

A student of mindfulness practices and Buddhist meditation for three decades, Mark Coleman has been teaching workshops and leading meditation retreats on five continents since 1997. Mark is a senior meditation teacher at Spirit Rock Meditation Center in Marin County, California.

Mark founded the Mindfulness Institute, which brings mindfulness training to Fortune 500 companies and nonprofit organizations across North America and Europe. Trained as a therapist, with an MA in clinical psychology, he also works as an executive coach and consultant. Mark is codirector of the Mindfulness Training Institute, where he leads mindfulness teacher trainings in the US and UK.

Mark is the author of *Awake in the Wild: Mindfulness in Nature as a Path of Self-Discovery*. An unabashed nature lover, Mark leads wilderness meditation retreats from Alaska to Peru through his organization Awake in the Wild. He is also a nature poet and has a poetry CD called *Poetry from the Wild*.

In addition, Mark is a master trainer for the Search Inside Yourself Leadership Institute, a Google-developed organization that provides mindfulness and emotional intelligence leadership

238 Make Peace with Your Mind

programs worldwide. He also codeveloped the course "Compassion, Presence, and Resilience Training: CPR-T" for healthcare practitioners. Mark is a leading contributor to whil.com, an online meditation platform.

Mark lives in Marin County, California, and enjoys spending his free time hiking, biking, kayaking, and exploring the great outdoors.

www.markcoleman.org
www.mindfulnessintheworld.com

NEW WORLD LIBRARY is dedicated to publishing books and other media that inspire and challenge us to improve the quality of our lives and the world.

We are a socially and environmentally aware company. We recognize that we have an ethical responsibility to our customers, our staff members, and our planet.

We serve our customers by creating the finest publications possible on personal growth, creativity, spirituality, wellness, and other areas of emerging importance. We serve New World Library employees with generous benefits, significant profit sharing, and constant encouragement to pursue their most expansive dreams.

As a member of the Green Press Initiative, we print an increasing number of books with soy-based ink on 100 percent postconsumer-waste recycled paper. Also, we power our offices with solar energy and contribute to non-profit organizations working to make the world a better place for us all.

Our products are available in bookstores everywhere.

www.newworldlibrary.com

At NewWorldLibrary.com you can download our catalog,
subscribe to our e-newsletter, read our blog,
and link to authors' websites, videos, and podcasts.

Find us on Facebook, follow us on Twitter, and watch us on YouTube.

Send your questions and comments our way!
You make it possible for us to do what we love to do.

Phone: 415-884-2100 or 800-972-6657
Catalog requests: Ext. 10 | Orders: Ext. 10 | Fax: 415-884-2199
escort@newworldlibrary.com

NEW WORLD LIBRARY
publishing books that change lives   14 Pamaron Way, Novato, CA 94949